Cyber Risk, Intellectual Property Theft and Cyberwarfare

The desire to steal the intellectual property (IP) of others, be they creative individuals or company teams working in patent pools to create new innovations, remains the same. Political methods have become more sophisticated in terms of devaluing the output of creative humans by creating open-source access, which can be taken freely by all and sundry. What has changed is the new cyber-based technology that allows increased theft of IP. Likewise, warfare for geo-political imperatives is not new but sophisticated cyber-based methods that can actually carry out infrastructural damage through cyberspace are new and are accordingly termed cyberwarfare. How cyber strategies are used in IP theft and cyberwarfare in relation to new complex digital technology such as the Internet of Things (IoT) is explored in relation to particular essential sectors in the economy: marine, smart energy power grids and insurance. Country-specific studies based on either being the recipient or perpetrator (or both) of cyberattacks provide analysis in relation to Japan, China and North Korea, Russia, Europe (the UK in particular), Iran and the USA.

Ruth Taplin (PhD LSE, Graduate Diploma in Law) is Editor of the *Interdisciplinary Journal of Economics and Business Law* (IJEBL), Author/Editor of 23 books and over 200 articles, Featured Author Routledge and Director of the Centre for Japanese and East Asian Studies.

Routledge Studies in the Growth Economies of Asia

139 Innovation, Investment and Intellectual Property in South Korea
Park to Park
Ruth Taplin

140 A Microcredit Alternative in South Asia
Akhuwat's experiment
Shahrukh Rafi Khan and Natasha Ansari

141 Development Agenda and Donor Influence in South Asia
Bangladesh's experiences in the PRSP regime
Mohammad Mizanur Rahman

142 How China's Silk Road Initiative is Changing the Global Economic Landscape
Edited by Yuan Li and Markus Taube

143 Trade Unions and Labour Movements in the Asia-Pacific Region
Edited by Byoung-Hoon Lee, Sek-Hong Ng and Russell Lansbury

144 International Entrepreneurship: A Comparative Analysis
Susan Freeman, Ying Zhu and Malcolm Warner

145 Ritual and Economy in Metropolitan China
A global social science approach
Carsten Herrmann-Pillath, Guo Man and Feng Xingyuan

146 Cyber Risk, Intellectual Property Theft and Cyberwarfare
Asia, Europe and the USA
Ruth Taplin

For more information about this series, please visit:
www.routledge.com/asianstudies/series/SE0133

Cyber Risk, Intellectual Property Theft and Cyberwarfare

Asia, Europe and the USA

Ruth Taplin

Routledge
Taylor & Francis Group
LONDON AND NEW YORK

First published 2021
by Routledge
2 Park Square, Milton Park, Abingdon, Oxon OX14 4RN

and by Routledge
605 Third Avenue, New York, NY 10017

First issued in paperback 2022

Routledge is an imprint of the Taylor & Francis Group, an informa business

Publisher's Note
The publisher has gone to great lengths to ensure the quality of this reprint but points out that some imperfections in the original copies may be apparent.

British Library Cataloguing-in-Publication Data
A catalogue record for this book is available from the British Library

Library of Congress Cataloging-in-Publication Data
A catalog record has been requested for this book

ISBN 13: 978-0-367-62185-8 (pbk)
ISBN 13: 978-1-138-32058-1 (hbk)
ISBN 13: 978-0-429-45319-9 (ebk)

DOI: 10.4324/9780429453199

Typeset in Times New Roman
by Newgen Publishing UK

Contents

Foreword

Cybersecurity in Australia – common global themes

Australia, like all countries, is well and truly engaged in the opportunity and challenge of cybersecurity. It is in the forefront of the minds of organisations, individuals and governments in figuring out how to best deal with a cyber-attack. Australia has sovereign capability and a mature approach to cybersecurity as well as an innovative eco-system to support companies and governments dealing with this new-age threat. In the case of the State of New South Wales there are cyber competitive advantages that are world leading such as Fin-tech, Ag-tech and a cyber skilled workforce.

New approaches and thinking are needed to address cybersecurity threats in a space where malicious actors are becoming more sophisticated, are using advanced capabilities in technologies and are global. Attacks are now using advanced artificial intelligence (AI), voice recognition, social media, big data and connected devices such as mobile phones to breach organisations and individuals. Strategic decision-making is required to allow for more informed investment and resourcing in order to enhance preparedness and resilience. Traditional ways to defend against cyber threats need to evolve and be implemented at an increasingly fast rate to keep pace with the advanced attacks that are occurring.

Cyber is an enabler not just a risk mitigation strategy. Traditionally, cybersecurity is seen as a risk mitigation tool used by information technology (IT) teams to try to stop and/or quickly mitigate a cyber breach. This view and approach is limiting the opportunities for an organisation to use data more proactively and enable new technologies and paradigms such as big data, AI, edge computing and automation. This is the opportunity for businesses and agencies to use cyber as an enabler and create value rather than as a cost centre.

In terms of how cyber breaches happen still, upwards of 70% of attacks occur because of human error such as opening a phishing e-mail. Increasingly, the phishing attacks are not just on laptop devices but hand-held devices too.

Cyber is primarily a people problem not an IT problem!

Used well cyber builds trust. If people and businesses don't trust you with their data they are not going to buy your product and you don't have a business. To build trust, you need to have a strong governance structure to support cyber initiatives. To assist in addressing this and as a first step, board and C-suite members as well as high-level policy-makers need to gain a better understanding of the cyber risks to which their organisation, municipality or country are exposed. This does not mean becoming full-on technical experts; technical expertise rests with the information and communications technology (ICT) and information security departments or contracted cybersecurity service providers. What urgently needs to improve is the communication and translation of cybersecurity issues between practitioners and leadership. Corporate leaders need to have a strong grasp of their entity's vulnerabilities and which critical assets are at risk. This will allow them to take timely strategic decisions on investment and resourcing to bolster their organisations' resilience and safeguards; a holistic approach needs to be used to be successful.

This type of thinking may require organisational restructures and governance in order to break down silos and enable a more robust cybersecurity attitude. Beyond economic losses, the legal, reputational and even physical consequences of a cyberattack can be huge. Leaders must create greater cyber-savviness across organisational functions such as risk, compliance, legal, human resources and communications, among others. A cybersecurity culture needs to be instilled across the organisation, from the top floor through to the shop floor.

New thinking may include deploying AI for threat detection and analysis as well as for incident response enabling more effective and efficient cybersecurity. At the same time, cybercriminals are adopting new technologies even faster and to their advantage. The developments in AI, quantum and identity management, among others, call for ever-greater investment to stay ahead of malicious actors. Needless to say, talent development also requires funding to build a strong cybersecurity-aware workforce.

Eco-system development and innovative partnerships are essential for not only addressing cybersecurity threats but in developing economic development outcomes. In a connected world it is essential that value is retained locally and high value-added jobs are being created and retained locally. In NSW (New South Wales) there is a strong and evolving cyber eco-system that consists of industry (private companies, small and medium-sized enterprises (SMEs) and non-governmental organisations (NGOs)), research, training providers including schools, vocational education and training, and government.

Key trends in cyber that will affect success and growth this year are discussed here.

AI will play an increasing role in both cyber-attack and defence

AI is the new way to get an edge over your opponents, but in an interconnected world anyone can get involved. Previously, governments could use this resource because of its expense, now everyone can use it. This means that while AI is undoubtedly being researched and developed, it's also easily used by parties with malicious intent.

So rather than between countries, today's race is between hackers, phishers and data thieves, and the experts in cybersecurity whose job it is to tackle those threats before they cause us harm. Just as AI can 'learn' to spot patterns of coincidence or behaviour that can signal an attempted attack, it can learn to adapt in order to disguise the same behaviour and trick its way past our defences. This added level of complexity also forms a geo-political threat between many state actors such as the US, Russia and China.

East and West lead to increased security threats

The internet and the online world is an international entity – relatively free of borders or restriction on the free movement of information and ideas. It's been built that way to leverage international cooperation and talent. In reality, the corporations, networks and associations that provide the infrastructure behind the scenes are legal entities obliged to comply with national laws and regulations.

Political interference is increasingly common and increasingly sophisticated

Targeted disinformation campaigns aimed at swaying public opinion have almost become an accepted feature of democracy today. So far, cybercrime targeting elections has taken two forms. The first involves the spreading of 'fake news' and false narratives – usually designed to slur a candidate – via social media. The second is direct attacks against candidates' or digital electoral infrastructure.

Countering the false narratives means building systems, either automated or manual, that can sift out lies, propaganda and bad-faith by analysing both content and metadata – where the information originates from, and who is likely to have created it.

The cybersecurity skills gap continues to grow

During 2020, it is projected the number of unfilled cybersecurity jobs will increase from just 1 million in 2014 to 3.5 million in Australia. This deficit of skills is likely to become a growing matter of public concern during the early part of this new decade. The threats we face in cyberspace today, from thieves attempting to clone identities to carry out fraud, to political disinformation campaigns designed to alter the course of democracies, will only become more intense unless there are sufficient people with the skills to counter them coming through the pipeline.

In NSW this is an area where significant work has been done creating a cyber talent accelerator that links areas of talent to business. A pipeline from schools, vocational education and training through to higher education has been created.

Automotive hacking, smart homes and data theft increases

Today, vehicles are basically moving data plants. Modern cars are fitted with an array of global positioning system (GPS) devices, sensors and in-car communication that make them an increasingly profitable target for hackers and data thieves. Likewise, this occurs in a modern home with an array of networked devices. In an interconnected world of technology, the IoT cannot be underestimated regarding how data theft could occur. More devices are constantly being added across the globe, adding to the complexity and options for data thieves.

Criminals have learned to piggyback into private networks through connected home appliances and smart devices thanks to the lack of security standards among the thousands of device manufacturers and service providers. Attackers will have the choice of targeting either vehicles or homes, perhaps using them to access e-mail accounts and then personal information, or the cloud services where our data are routinely sent for storage and analysis. Large-scale harvesting and resale of these data on the black market is highly lucrative for cybercriminals.

Increasing cyberwarfare

The goal of cyberwarfare is to 'weaken, disrupt or destroy' an enemy target. These targets could be attacked either by a nation-state or Denial of Service (DoS) attacks. Cyberwarfare threats range from propaganda to espionage and serious disruption with loss of life and extensive infrastructure disruption. These types of cyberattacks are disrupting governments and societies in a high-impact way that we have never seen before. They constitute the future of warfare globally.

Finally, with all these growing cyber risks, this book by Ruth Taplin is both timely and much needed to explain all the above aspects of a future of increased cyberattack and how we need to deal with such events globally. If we do not heed these warnings, all of us will be the losers. As noted in research by Coveware, the average ransomware payment in the fourth quarter has increased from US$ 41,198 in the third quarter to US$84,116 in the US in 2019.[1]

Furthermore, cyberattacks are taking a physical form as an Israeli cybersecurity firm identified a new type of ransomware that it believes was created by Iran to lock up or even delete industrial control systems as happened at Bahrain Petroleum Co.[2]

To counter cyber risk and cyberattack whether it be financial, BI, physical infrastructure or reputational attack, it is vital to have local experts involved, cooperation and sharing of information between those under cyberattack, experts who understand the complexity of IoT and a book such as this one that will point those under cyberattack in the right direction to both understand and deal with these cybersecurity issues.

Todd Williams
Director, NSW Cyber Security Node
New South Wales, Australia

Notes

1 'Average ransomware payment jumped 104 percent in the fourth quarter', Erin Ayers, *Advisen Cyber News* (31 January 2020).
2 'Cyberattacks linked to Iran appear to target Bahrain Petroleum Co.', Erin Ayers, *Advisen Cyber News* (31 January 2020).

Acknowledgements

The author would like thank a number of colleagues for their assistance with this book. They include Prof. Motohiro Tsuchiya of Keio University, Prof. Akio Nishizawa of Toyo University, Mr Akio Ono of Japan Subway Association and Mr James Brewer, former insurance editor of *Lloyd's List* for invaluable shipping and insurance expertise. Dr Jacob Mendel for his PhD smart grids material and Prof. Tad Kowalski of Poznan University must also be thanked for assistance with Eastern European and smart grids material.

The Great Britain Sasakawa Foundation for their travel grant to make my research visit to Japan in March/April 2019 a reality.

Peter Sowden, Routledge Editor, for his continuing wise words. We would like to thank the late Elisabet Ainsworth (née Sinkie) who was production manager at Routledge for most of my books. She will be sorely missed.

Cyber glossary[1]

Back door	An entry that is hidden to the computer bypassing logins and passwords
Big data	Very large data sets used computationally to detect patterns and trends
Black hat	This refers to villains in Hollywood Westerns who wore grey or black hats vis-à-vis the good white hats, the former meaning illegal hackers who are usually involved in pecuniary gain
Botnet	A network of devices controlled by hackers
Bots	These are computer-generated programmes that masquerade as humans
Brute force attack	Automated search for every possible password permutation
Business interruption	A cyberattack with the sole intention of destroying the normal flow of business activities
BYOD	Bring Your Own Device
Cracking	Attempted break-in of a secure system
DDoS	Distributed Denial of Service
DoS	Denial of Service
Doxing	Tracing the digital footprint of an internet user and then making it public
Dragonfly	It uses two types of malware – both are Remote Access Tool, which provides hackers access and control to compromised computers. Its preferred malware tool is Backdoor.Oldrea, which acts as a backdoor for hackers to extract data and insert more malware
Grey hat	Someone hacking and breaking the law for a non-pecuniary reason such as a political one or personal grudge against an employer and often in the anonymous hacker grouping
Honeypot	This is when a trap is set, for example an information system that appears to be part of the system with

	valuable information stored, while in reality it has no connection to the actual system. It is used to detect and deflect hackers
Identity theft	Impersonation of real people and organisations through fraudulently having obtained their details online and then trying to extract money, mortgage details and so forth to steal for financial gain or to ruin reputation
Internet protocol address	This is a device's fingerprint that can be used to track the person using it, their location or activity
IoT	Internet of Things – meaning all product devices that are interconnected and can be subject to control through the internet
ISP	Internet service provider
Keystroke logging	Tracking by keys being pressed on a computer to record passwords and login details in general
LAN	Local Area Network
Malspam	Malware delivered through e-mail messeages
Malware	A *mal*icious soft*ware* programme that is designed to steal data, or damage a device. Variants include viruses, spyware, Trojans and other abusive injections into a computing system
Metadata	Data that give information regarding other data
Misconfigurations	Interference in configurations in devices such as disrupting the ability of firewalls to detect which is a trusted or untrusted portion of a network
MITM	Man-in-the-Middle whereby the hackers insert themselves in between the victim and intended party during communication to intercept, view and change sensitive data
Node	An individual system within the blockchain that stores the entire blockchain ledger
Phishing	Fraudulently tricking users of digital devices into giving the cybercriminal personal information such as credit card details, passwords and online banking details. This is often done by imitating e-mails from genuine organisations. This is targeted at groups such as finance departments
QoS	Quality of Service.
Reputational loss	An attempt through identity theft and business interruption to ruin the reputation of a company to malicious effect

Scanning	Attacking large portions of the internet at random. Targeted attacks can be more sophisticated using or creating tools specifically for a targeted attack on a company or ship. Such a technique could be **social engineering**, which is a non-technical approach that manipulates insiders to break security procedures, usually initiated through social media but not exclusively
Script kiddie	A description of a hacker who lacks technical skills
Secure Shell (SSH)	Protocol for connecting to a server enabling file transfers, for example
Side channel attacks	These are targeted to retrieve confidential information from a smart grid's critical infrastructure equipment such as passwords and cryptographic keys
Spear-phishing	This is the same as phishing but targeted at individuals with a group
Spoofing	Altering an e-mail so it appears to be originated from an organisation such as a person's bank or insurance company
Spyware	A malware programme that sends back information while hiding in a computer
SQL	Structured query language is similar to a code injection attack in that it inserts new code into vulnerable software to change the information or flow of execution
Stuxnet	The first malware developed solely for the purposes of targeting industrial control systems such as a power plant or gas pipeline
Trojan horse	Malware that masquerades as useful software while installing a back door into a user's computer
TSA	Time sychronisation attack, which targets the timing information of, for example, a smart grid
Viruses	Self-replicating malware that continues to reproduce itself inside a user's computer while destroying hard drives, stealing data and logging into keystrokes
VPN	Virtual Private Network
WAN	Wide Area Network
Water holing	Establishing a fake website or compromising a genuine website to exploit visitors
Whaling	Phishing that targets the upper management of companies for either pecuniary gain or wider exposure for the political cause of the hacker

White hat	An ethical hacker who uses their digital skills for social good and/or assists organisations to overcome vulnerabilities in their computing systems
Zero-day	The threat of an unknown cybersecurity vulnerability

Note

1 Most of these definitions are taken from my previous books such as Ruth Taplin (ed.), *Managing Cyber Risk in Financial Institutions: Lessons from Asia, Europe and the US*, Abingdon: Routledge, 2016. Other sources are fully attributed within the book.

Abbreviations

ACE	Academic Centre of Excellence
ACORD	Association for Cooperative Operations Research and Development
AGCS	Allianz Global Corporate and Speciality
AI	artificial intelligence
AIS	Automatic Identification System
ASEAN	Association of Southeast Asian Nations
AT&T	American Telephone and Telegraph
BI	business interruption
BIMCO	Baltic and International Maritime Council
BT	British Telecom
CISTA	Collective Intelligent Agents for Trusted Advocates
COMAC	Commercial Aircraft Corporation of China
CSC	Cyber Security Council
CVC	Card Verification Code
DARPA	Defense Advanced Research Projects Agency
DCMS	(UK Department for) Digital, Culture, Media and Sport
DDoS	Distributed Denial of Service
DHS	Department of Homeland Security
DISA	Defense Information Systems Agency
DNC	Democratic National Committee
DoJ	Department of Justice
DoS	Denial of Service
EBR	*Economics and Business Review*
EPSRC	Engineering and Physical Sciences Research Council
EU	European Union
FBI	Federal Bureau of Investigation
FS-ISAC	Financial Services Information Sharing and Analysis Center
GCHQ	Government Communications Headquarters
GDPR	Global Data Protection Regulation
GPS	global positioning system
IACS	International Association of Classification Societies
ICT	information and communications technology

IISE	Institute for International Socio-Economic Studies
IMO	International Maritime Organization
IoT	Internet of Things
IP	intellectual property
IPA	Information-technology Protection Agency
IPR	intellectual property rights
ISM	International Safety Management
ISP	internet service provider
IT	information technology
IUA	International Underwriting Association
JPCERT/CC	Japan Computer Emergency Response Team/ Coordination Center
LOC	London Offshore Consultants
METI	Ministry of Economy, Trade and Industry
MGA	Managing General Agent
MoD	Ministry of Defence
MTEU	Million Twenty-foot Equivalent Unit
NAIC	National Association of Insurance Commissioners
NATO	North Atlantic Treaty Organization
NCSC	National Cyber Security Centre (UK)
NDAA	National Defense Authorization Act
NGO	non-governmental organisation
NICT	National Institute of Information and Communications Technology
NISC	National Information Security Center
NIST	National Institute of Standards and Technology
NSA	National Security Agency
NSF	National Science Foundation
NSM	Norwegian National Security Authority
NSW	New South Wales
OT	operations technology
P&C	property and casualty
P&I	protection and indemnity
PC	personal computer
PRA	Prudential Regulation Authority
PRC	People's Republic of China
PwC	PriceWaterhouseCoopers
R&D	research and design
RFID	Radio-Frequency Identification
RUSI	Royal United Services Institute
SEC	Security Exchange Commission
SME	small and medium-sized enterprise
SORM	System of Operative Search Measures
SSH	Secure Shell
TEU	Twenty-foot Equivalent Unit

TF	Task Force
UN	United Nations
USCG	United States Coast Guard
VTMAS	Vessel Traffic Management System
VTS	Vessel Traffic Service
WMD	weapons of mass destruction
WTO	World Trade Organization

1 Introduction

The desire to steal the intellectual property (IP) of others, be they creative individuals or company teams working in patent pools to create new innovations, has not changed. Political methods have become more sophisticated in terms of devaluing the output of creative humans by creating open-source access,[1] which can be taken freely by all and sundry. There was furore, for example, after an Open Access Library opened in San Francisco, California that on its own accord stocked well-known books without author permission or intention to recognise or compensate the authors with royalties. It was only when the biggest name authors threatened to sue that it took notice. This also happens with well-known inventors. The renowned British inventor James Dyson won £4 million from Hoover, a vacuum cleaner competitor,[2] for infringing a Dyson patent, but believes he would have lost the case if his company had been smaller. The other major way to deprive creative people of their rewards for original thinking and innovativeness is through cyberattack, which is on the increase globally and needs to be addressed as this book does. The theft of IP through cyberattack for whatever motivation must not be underestimated. In fact, the new 'tsars' of the digital age such as those who founded Napster, Facebook and Google wish to have the same control or even more than the corporate capitalists they criticise when it comes to profiting from content creators and the creative process. Sean Parker who founded Napster was one of the earliest examples of someone who created software that digitally extracted the music content of CDs and allowed up to 70 million users to share it on computer networks for free. Parker knew he was breaking copyright law and stealing IP from music content creators. Eventually record companies filed a legal challenge to this blatant copyright infringement and shut Napster down in July 2001. Sean Parker had no regrets becoming a convicted corporate hacker revelling in the fact that he was the inventor of the first technology to steal IP. As shown in the film *The Social Network* (about Facebook), Parker was eventually appointed President of Facebook by Mark Zuckerberg, the founder of Facebook. Larry Page, the founder and CEO of Google, never had the talent to become a saxophonist or a composer of music so he moved to computer science eventually founding Google. When setting up the governance of this digital corporation Page and his partner at Google Sergei Brin, organised a two-tier stockholder system in which they had ten times the voting power of those who bought publicly offered shares. As Page explained in his first letter to shareholders, 'new investors will fully share in Google's long-term economic future but will have little ability to influence its strategic decisions through their voting rights'. The underlying philosophy seems to be that it is fine to take creative content without asking permission as Google copied the entire content of the world wide web and indexed it without asking anyone's permission. This all follows on from Page's initial creation of software to extract music content from CDs infringing copyright and stealing IP without permission from anyone.[3]

It is not surprising then that hackers and proponents of digital-age corporations such as Napster, Facebook and Google find the stealing of IP and denying the genuine creators of content royalties a natural course of events in the same way as those who support open access. These tendencies are related to other web-based social malaise such as not respecting the private nature of data collection or the interference in the outcomes of elections. This has led to the founder of the world wide web Sir Tim Berners-Lee to battle 'digital dystopia' and call for greater regulation and certain standards to be instituted. In November 2019 he proposed through his World Wide Web Foundation a Contract for the Web that would stop election interference by foreign powers, hate speech, abuse of privacy and disinformation.[4]

As my *Managing Cyber Risk in the Financial Sector* book noted, when planning to mitigate cyber risk the centre of the enquiry should not be prevention based on statistical modelling or solely on IT packages but on the human-based variables. Hackers cannot steal IP or alter GPS systems connected to ship navigation without human ignorance/error, collusion, grudges, greed, malice and geo-political imperatives. Therefore, it is important to understand not only how the technology works, such as the multi-connections of Internet of Things (IoT) devices that allow through interconnectivity so many more ways for hackers to exploit the weaknesses in so many connections to enter the cyber system, but also it is essential to understand the human motivation for the hacking. It is also crucial to look internally in an organisation to find those with a motivation to carry out cyberattacks to undermine the system without being caught. In an increasingly complex world and particularly with cyberwarfare, we must assess the motivations of the very human global players behind the cyberattacks. Likewise, in a company it is essential to train staff and customers as well as managers in SME supply chains. Those that supply goods to the larger companies are the weakest links because of their lack of human resources. Larger companies are usually the best prepared to counter cyberattack because of an abundance of resources, both human and technological due to economy of scale.

IP theft

As Mike Pompeo, the US Secretary of State noted[5] in relation to the current trade problems with China, IP theft is at the heart of most cyber risk/attack problems. 'China steals intellectual property for military purposes,' he said. 'It wants to dominate AI, space technology, ballistic missiles and many other areas.'

This could not be a truer statement as my research visit in March/April 2019 to Japan for this book showed that the greatest cyber risk/attack issues revolve around IP theft. A Japanese survey that took place in 2018 and was published the following year by the prestigious Institute for International Socio-Economic Studies (IISE) showed IP theft to be highest in Japan when looking at institutional targets of cyberattack – 25% in Japan compared to 10% in Asia as a whole and 12% globally. This is why we focus on Japan in this book as IP theft is extraordinarily high. Globally, IP theft is highest in the US, the UK and Western Europe. According to this IISE survey, business interruption (BI) was the main target of cyberattacks on organisations, globally at 30%, in Asia at 27%, while in Japan at 17%. These differences are very significant for assessing the reasons why IP theft is under-studied and why its impact targets few but economically significant countries with often crippling effects. BI can also be crippling for business and government organisations but can be restored, while theft of IP cannot be regained without devastating effects for the organisation or individuals.[6] Interestingly, the occurrences of targeted cyberattack for geo-political or state reasons is at 6% for Japan and Asia and 5% globally, which is much less significant compared to the media attention it receives.[7] Yet, in industries such as the maritime sector or insurance, which are global in nature due to international trade, state/geo-political cyberattacks are increasing.

IP vulnerability

It is the intangible aspects of IP that makes it so vulnerable to cyber risk and attack affecting business and trade relations worldwide. It can operate at a number of levels and in all types of industries as this book will demonstrate. Levels include industry, government, military defence establishments and businesses of all sizes. The geo-political, trade sectors and finance including banking and insurance are all prey to this 21st-century digital-age menace. Some industries are more prone to IP theft, cyberattack and potential/variants of cyberwarfare, often in unexpected ways, such as shipping, national grids, defence systems and retail banking systems. Examples as in previous books are mainly from Japan, Europe and the USA but in terms of the shipping sector, for instance, it can occur anywhere in the world because of global trade routes.

Cyber risk/attack and IP theft are very broad topics that touch most aspects of our lives but often most of us are not even aware of them or the remedies for dealing with them occurring at all different levels. For example, in the insurance industry, which through underwriting should cover a wide range of cyber risk, is only now dealing with silent cyber risk. Two new London Market model clauses to help underwriters manage cyber losses have been published by the International Underwriting Association (IUA). The wordings have been developed in order to address issues of non-affirmative or 'silent' cover, where traditional insurance policies may unintentionally suggest protection for undefined cyber risks. The importance of wordings cannot be underestimated as explained in my presentation book launch of *Managing Cyber Risk in the Financial Sector* in the City of London on 16 March 2016 supported by the IUA. I stated that:

> Insurers were left in a difficult position because of the dearth of facts and detail. We are dealing with a new phenomenon where people do not even know the language to use to describe cyberattack, and how can you deal with something when you do not share a common language?

Since then definitions of cyber words used in insurance documents have moved forward.[8]

First, a Cyber Loss Absolute Exclusion Clause (reference: IUA 09-081) provides market participants with an option to exclude in the broadest possible manner any loss arising from the use of a computer system, network or data – each of which is clearly defined. Meanwhile, a Cyber Loss Limited Exclusion Clause (reference: IUA 09-082) enables only the exclusion of losses directly caused by cyber events, rather than 'directly or indirectly'.

Chris Jones, IUA director of legal and market services, said:

> These two new model clauses provide broad policy exclusions which may be utilised as a starting or reference point for underwriters offering cover for traditional business classes that may include an element of cyber risk. By developing class-specific write backs insurers can then explicitly state the extent of any cover provided for such losses.

Both clauses were developed in response to concerns expressed by the Prudential Regulation Authority (PRA) about potentially unintended or unclear provision of coverage for cyber risks in various classes of insurance business. The issue was addressed by the regulator in a November 2016 consultation paper ('Cyber insurance underwriting risk') and subsequent policy statement (PS 15/17). Companies were urged to actively manage their exposures by considering adjustments to premiums, robust wording exclusions and specific limits of cover.

Mr Jones added:

> Silent cyber cover creates uncertainty for both insurers and clients and has been a hot topic in the London company market for some time now.

> Increasing regulatory scrutiny has, of course, further highlighted the issue, but IUA members have been considering different approaches even before it was first raised by the PRA.
>
> Many traditional policies were designed when cyber wasn't a major risk and often do not explicitly mention cyber. Some high-profile cyber events and losses have clearly demonstrated, however, how important it is to address.[9]

Awareness and concern of companies of all sizes of cyber risk, and how it affects their business and insurance needs has been highlighted recently by global professional services firm Aon plc, which released its Cyber Captive Survey 2019 Report entitled *Creating Value for the Cyber Risk Agenda*, which shows an increase in demand for cyber products among captive owners who have bought such cover in the past.

As captive insurance companies were set up by parent companies to cover risks that were not widely covered by mainstream insurance companies and that were too costly because companies required stable pricing, it is apposite to note that captives are providing cyber-risk cover at an accelerated rate with increasing demand.

This report reveals current attitudes and trends among captive buyers of cyber insurance that include global insights into the ongoing challenges and opportunities for captive owners seeking to manage cyber risk. It also highlights the growing need for cyber-risk cover and sectoral demand:

- The growth in gross written premium for cyber risks within the captive market has accelerated in the last year by 263% year on year.
- The industries buying most cyber cover within a captive are Healthcare (19%) and Energy (15%).
- The range in limits of cover taken out is up to US$ 100,000 million.
- The percentage of captives surveyed that are incubating cyber risk has reached 41%.
- The percentage of captives that are having BI cover wording within their cyber policies has reached 63%. This reflects the IISE study mentioned above emphasising BI being the most frequent purpose of cyberattack among organisations globally.
- Captives that have suffered a cyber loss has reached 26% and 29% of losses have been a full-limit loss.
- Greater control of insurance programmes (37%) and achieving cost efficiencies (37%) are the two main reasons for captive use of cyber risks.
- It is estimated that 34% of all captives will be underwriting cyber in five years' time.

John English, CEO, Captive and Insurance Management, Aon, said:

> Captives continue to play a valuable role in addressing emerging risk issues for all companies. Our survey demonstrates that a captive not only can provide access to innovative coverage and unlock additional capacity for

> this fast moving risk topic, but also better coordinate key internal teams in a company to improve overall capital allocation, strategic planning, and risk improvement for cyber risk.

Adam Peckman, Global Practice Leader, Cyber Solutions, Aon, said:

> Driven by the digital economy, Cyber remains one of the most critical risks facing all global businesses; however, this survey found that management of cyber risk remains largely fragmented and inconsistent across corporate functions.
>
> It is critical that cyber risk is treated as an enterprise risk and framed within the existing risk management framework. Risk Managers can lead this change by utilising captives as a key strategic tool to demystify cyber risk through more sophisticated analysis and drive more fit-for-purpose balance sheet protection.[10]

Such needs for cyber-risk insurance including the coverage of intellectual property rights (IPR) theft will be explored in this book.

Who is carrying out IPR theft?

Who is carrying out these cyberattacks that impact IPR as the hackers collect unauthorised data? The US Justice Department unsealed an indictment of two Chinese nationals in 2019, charging them with the 2014 hack of the insurance company Anthem and attacks on three other, unnamed American businesses the following year.

The charges were the latest in a string of aggressive moves by American officials who say they are trying to crack down on the theft of trade secrets and personal data by China.

A federal grand jury in Indianapolis, where Anthem is based, charged Fujie Wang, 32, of Shenzhen, China, and an individual indicted as John Doe with conspiring to commit fraud, wire fraud and intentional damage to a protected computer.

The indictment says the two targeted employees of an Anthem subsidiary and at least three other companies with so-called spear-phishing e-mails beginning on 18 February 2014. Less than a month later, the indictment says, the hackers got inside Anthem's network and searched through troves of personal data.

By January 2015, the indictment states, the hackers had obtained nearly 80 million records, including Social Security numbers, birth dates, postal/e-mail addresses and employment and income information for Anthem customers and employees, including Anthem's chief executive.

The attack, which the company disclosed in February 2015, and a hack of the federal Office of Personnel Management, which disclosed a significant breach four months later, marked a turning point in Chinese cyberespionage.

Previously, Chinese hackers had been largely focused on stealing American trade secrets – everything from Benjamin Moore's formula for paint to blueprints of stealth bombers. But with the attacks on Anthem and the Office of Personnel Management, Chinese hackers demonstrated new interest in the personal data of Americans, particularly government employees.

After those two breaches, other businesses that hold large collections of personal data began reporting that they had been targeted. The list included other major insurers; Equifax, the large credit reporting bureau; hospitality companies such as the Marriott Hotel Group; and airlines such as British Airways.[11]

The stolen data never appeared on the so-called dark web, where criminals trade it for identity theft and other schemes – suggesting that the attackers had a motive other than profit.

Security researchers and government officials said they believed that the stolen data were being stockpiled. It could be used for a number of purposes, including rooting out spies and their collaborators.

The Chinese authorities could, for example, look at hotel reservations to see if people they suspected of espionage stayed in the same city at the same time. They could also use sensitive health and financial data for blackmail.[12]

A Senate hearing had staff from the FBI (Federal Bureau of Investigation) testifying that they wished they had acted more quickly to stop Chinese recruiting US researchers to steal IP from laboratories on a large scale.

John Brown, Assistant Director of the Counterintelligence Division of the FBI, confirmed the findings of a Senate subcommittee report that a delay in action by federal agencies allowed China to recruit the researchers with the result that US taxpayers inadvertently actually funded the rise of the Chinese military and economy. He stated: 'With our present-day knowledge of the threat from Chinese plans, we wish we had taken more rapid and comprehensive action in the past.' Brown added, 'The time to make up for that is now.'

This IP theft occurred despite China's announcement in 2008 of the Thousand Talents Plan in which China had originally planned to recruit some 2,000 people but ended up recruiting more than 7,000 by 2017. In spite of these warnings the FBI did not respond with any gravitas until 2018.

Part of the current trade war between the US and China rests with Washington's demands and dismay that China has been using a number of illicit methods as described below to take a short cut to advance technologically at the expense of the US. The Chinese government, in turn, has denied allegations of espionage and has said actual cases of those prosecuted for such offences are politically motivated and exaggerated.

Senators also asked officials from the National Science Foundation, the National Institutes of Health, and the Department of Energy and State Department as to what can be done to counter China's stealing of IP from the US. Senator Maggie Hassan stated: 'I hope very much that this is one of the first steps we take in developing a real national strategy in combating this because clearly China has a strategy, and we need one of our own.'

Senators Rob Portman, the Republican subcommittee chairman, and Tom Carper, its top Democrat, noted they would use the report to write legislation to end 'this abuse' of US research, IP and taxpayer money funding it.[13]

The European Union (EU) issued a report in October 2019 warning without mentioning any names that a country hostile to the interests of the EU could use its 5G telecoms infrastructure to create havoc through cyberattacks at every level of the political economy and society. Yet, the implication pointed to Chinese telecommunications giant Huawei, which has been banned by the US for exactly these cyber risks.[14] To date, Huawei will not be asked to participate in 5G development in the UK.

However, it is not just external enemies from foreign companies/countries who use cyberattacks to obtain stolen IP. In the US people who commit such espionage are seen to be motivated by other drivers. US officials who have studied the crime of espionage created an acronym that establishes motives: MICE (money, ideology, compromise and ego). Seeming American patriots such as suburban based Kevin Mallory are typical of those recruited by Chinese agents to steal US trade secrets for them.[15]

Russia is the other significant land of hackers who steal IP, trade secrets and data. The Bank of Lithuania noted that cybercrime poses the greatest risk to its domestic financial system.[16] This is why a small country such as Lithuania in 2019 ranked fourth after the UK, the US and France in cyber preparedness having installed a network of comprehensive cybersecurity systems and relying on innovation to find cyber solutions. It was ranked in 2017 by the United Nations (UN) Survey as 57th for cybersecurity readiness. Since then, it is leading an EU initiative to create a cyber rapid response force.[17]

Cyberwarfare definitions and directions

Yet again warfare is not a new subject but unfortunately part of the human condition since time immemorial. The essence of human warfare is a relentless quest for power and domination over others whether they be nations, tribes or individuals. Warfare also involves theft of the resources, material objects, property in any form and even happiness of others targeted. However, conventional warfare is becoming a relic of the past to be replaced by cyberwarfare. As General Sir Nick Carter, the Chief of the Defence Staff in the UK has stated, Britain is 'at war every day' due to constant cyberattacks from Russia and elsewhere. He further noted that distinctions between peace and war 'don't exist any longer' in the modern world and that

> I feel I am now at war, but it's not a war in the way we would have defined it in the past. And that is because great power competition and the battle of ideas with non-state actors is threatening us on a daily basis.

General David Petraeus, former Director of the CIA and retired United States Army General, supports General Carter in viewing the future of warfare being waged online. He also believes cyberwarfare is being increasingly driven by China and Russia. He sees China's unprecedented rise as a major power in the last 40 years coupled with Russia's revanchist tendencies are the drivers in changing international norms concerning global warfare. He credits Russia with forcing NATO (North Atlantic Treaty Organization) to modernise and to understand that future warfare will take place in cyberspace and actual space.

General Carter concurred that both China and Russia have broken the legal and ethical basis of what was known as armed conflict. He acknowledged that future warfare will become information-centric with control and manipulation of information at the core of any conflict.[18]

Cyberwarfare and insurance

The insurance industry is again reflecting current reality when trying to define the nature of cyberattack. A new report by Capsicum Reinsurance makes it clear that the insurance industry will not be able to rely on traditional methods for determining whether cyberattacks should be considered acts of war. The report suggests that cyber should be viewed as a peril and from that starting point decide how to insure it within the warfare context.[19]

Cyberwarfare and political interference

Russia is using a new type of cyberwarfare that adds a new dimension to the definition of warfare. It is using a hughly effective form of political and disinformation warfare that is much more effective than conventional warfare. It targets very specific political weaknesses such as elections and leaves the rest such as banks or infrastructure alone. This way Russian hackers can expend as little time and money without killing a single person or causing obvious physical damages, leaving the leader of a country to carry out policies favourable to Russia without being detected. Cyberattacks involving disinformation are indirect, difficult to trace and can be moved from one platform to another quickly.

This is reflected in current concerns about the forthcoming 2020 elections in the US. The 2016 elections were more supportive of the Republicans with Trump as their leader due to concerted Russian interference through social media. This ranged from disinformation frightening voters with false descriptions of Hilary Clinton's bad behaviour and untrustworthy character to non-existent Americans giving testimony why voters should not vote for Clinton. There is concern that in not providing all political party candidates in the US a cybersecurity fund that provides cyber protection against such Russian-backed political cyberwarfare attacks will again bias the election against the Democrats. The attempt to provide such cybersecurity funding to all running for election was squashed by Mitch McConnell, the Republican leader of the Senate who supports the idea that individuals and parties should provide their own cybersecurity. It is increasingly clear that the costs of hiring private cybersecurity companies for electoral fairness is way beyond the means of most political parties and individuals.

In Britain, the Army has been recruited to wage a cyberwar against Russian political interference, such as false items on social media that disparage the effectiveness of the Army, by deploying soldiers to work on social media to block such potentially damaging interference. Lieutenant General Ivan Jones, Commander of the Field Army, will be using his forces to counter malign Russian influence and that of terrorist groups such as Isil digitally through social media.[20]

Cyberwarfare IP theft

Yet, a non-political but physically damaging form of cyberwarfare can become a reality and is linked to IP theft. The *Washington Post* reported in 2018 that the Chinese state hacked into an American Naval contractor and stole a significant amount of very sensitive data related to submarine warfare.[21]

Cybermercenaries

A new type of mercenary is emerging alongside the advent of cyberwarfare. This is the cybermercenary for hire to carry out acts of computerised warfare. War is being outsourced and privatised to a new group of cybermercenaries. The attraction of cybermercenaries for nation-states is that they can be used as non-state actors who are difficult to trace especially when doing the 'dirty work' the state wants to distance itself from such as the Russian hackers cyberattack in 2015 on the Ukranian government's IT systems, which caused hudreds of millions of dollars damage worldwide. Cyber hackers for hire can implicate others and cover their tracks more easily as they can move from one country to another rapidly and often without trace.[22]

In the conflict with Iran there is growing evdence that the US is moving away from coventional warfare methods to use a more two-pronged hybrid form of cyberwarfare. The US had all conventional methods of warfare attack ready but stopped it short of ten minutes of air strikes being launched in retalitaion for the destruction of a US$ 130 million drone in international waters of the Straits of Hormuz and attacks on non-Iranian oil tankers in the area for which the US had pictures and Iran denied responsibility. The US then launched cyberattacks instead. The goal was to develop operations similar to the shadow war the US has accused Tehran of carrying out through cyberattacks directed at the US by the Iranian Revolutionary Guards Corps.

The cyberattacks were targeted at an Iranian intelligence group that American officials believe was behind the series of attacks on tankers and was intended to shut down the computers and networks used by the intelligence group, even temporarily. Another separate online operation was aimed at destroying computers that control Iranian missile launches. This shadow hybrid warfare uses indirect means through cyber and actual physical attack to, for example, make insurance premiums, this time Lloyd's, excessively high in the Persian Gulf region upon which the US and Europe as well as Japan depend on for oil.[23] Iran in June 2019 had been using hackers, most likely government sponsored, to cyberattack US government agencies and key economic sectors such as oil, gas and finance by sending waves of phishing e-mails according to cybersecurity companies such as CrowdStrike and FireEye.[24]

Sectoral targets of cyberattack

In this book we will also look at different industrial sectors increasingly affected by cyberattack, which has implications for IP theft and cyberwarfare. Power grids are the most often attacked followed by oil and gas. The latter has complex systems of networks and physical infrastructure globally. It is often hostile states that are the main perpetrators of such attacks but it can also be other types of hackers who are interested in extorting money. The attack on the Saudi Arabian Aramco oil installations was an early incident of cyberwarfare.[25]

Shipping and aviation sectors

Although it would appear that the avaiation sector should be a prime target of cyberattack, it has been less of a target than the marine sector, for example. This has been the case largely because of the very strict security at airports that was tightened substantially since the 9/11 terrorist attacks that took place in 2001 in the US. Yet, a recent report by the Atlantic Council in the US argues that the aviation industry has a good deal of work to do in relation to pilot training and information sharing.[26]

The shipping industry has long underemphasised its vulnerability but is realising its susceptability to cyberattack in recent years. According to a new report from Allianz Global Corporate and Speciality (AGCS), the shipping industry is acknowledging that events such as the NotPetya attack of June 2017 has put at risk not only safety but also operations and revenue of maritime trade upon which all global industrial trade is reliant.[27]

Another sector that is increasingly vulnerable is medical/healthcare (as mentioned in my last book on the subject *Managing Cyber Risk in the Financial Sector*). A medical testing company in the US, Labcorp, reported a 7.7 million customer personel and financial data breach. The breach occurred through a third-party billing collections agency company.[28]

Cyber theft of IPR can also take the form of very longstanding disputes between telecoms companies, for example over design or patent theft. The Qualcomm, Samsung and Apple iPhone disputes have been some of the longest running in the industry. They have been covered in many of my previous books (see *Managing Cyber Risk and the Financial Sector* for example) but amazingly are still continuing and will be analysed within this book.

A recent dispute over alleged patent theft has Huawei, which is one of China's largest technology companies, accusing the US telecoms company Verizon of infringing 238 of its patents. The problem is complex because Verizon does not buy any wireless or networking products off Huawei but uses 20 vendors who do use Huawei technology. Huawei is trying to force Verizon to pay its licensing fees, which could amount to one billion dollars. This request for licensing fees by Huawei could be linked to China's threat of retribution against US telecoms/IT companies if they follow President Trump's ban on using Huawei's products because they are a security risk to the US, a claim that is ostensibly linked to Chinese cyberattacks and theft of US IPR, especially in the defence industry.[29]

Cyber and state control

Cyber theft of IP and cyberwarfare is increasingly not only used by countries against foreign adversaries who they wish to undermine but also against their own population they wish to control. In Hong Kong from 12 to 14 June 2019 a massive protest occurred challenging a new extradition bill that was to be passed by the Hong Kong legislature, which would mean in real terms anyone deemed a 'criminal' in Hong Kong could be extradited to Mainland China. Protestors wary of being silenced with no access to independent legal aid if extradicted used their mobiles and the secure Telegram app to communicate the details of where and when the protest would be held. China bombarded the Telegram app to disrupt communication between the protestors.[30]

Another area that can be attacked causing limited but severe infrastructural damage are the electrical grids that every major city has to power light, heat, air conditioning and many other essentials. This is another target for cyberattack often by Russia and rogue states such as North Korea.

The importance of power grids is becoming more complex as they transform to smart grids. Jacob Mendel describes a smart grid as a system that integrates traditional electrical power networks with communications and information digital technology. This comprehensive system that can manage itself is becoming more vulnerable to cyberattack that can amount to a form of cyberwarfare. Many countries such as those in the EU, the United States and India are digitising their energy infrastructure, which means that they are also being required to develop cybersecurity measures to counteract the possible hacking into such essential economic infrastructure. The costs therefore are very high if such a cyberattack is successful, not only in monetary costs to be borne by the electric company and taxpayers but also in terms of the electric company's reputation, IPR and loss of data to name a few consequential losses. Therefore, many countries by necessity are developing cybersecurity tools and frameworks to deal with such potentially catastrophic cyberattacks.[31]

Yet, recently, it has been the US that is attacking Russia's power grid. In June 2019, the US increased its digital incursions into targeting Russia's electrical power grid. This cyberattack was felt acutely at a heating power plant in Moscow. This has occurred after years of warnings issued by the FBI and the Department of Homeland Security (DHS) that a Cold War retaliation would ensue if Russia did not stop inserting malware into US computers that could sabotage US power grids, water supplies and oil and gas pipelines. The Russians were able as early as 2008 to begin this Cold War cyberwarfare by dropping USBs infected with malware in the car parking lot of an American base in a Middle Eastern country. US personnel picked them up and inserted them into their computers. The US Cyber Command was born out of this USB malware infected strategy aided by human personnel thoughtlessness and error. This was the same year that the Chinese hacked into Lockheed Martin, the aerospace designer and manufacturer, to steal their IP designs of the F-35 fighter jet. Today China has built a fighter jet very similar to the F-35.[32]

These are cyberwarfare attacks on the military and defence manufacturers but in 27 April 2007 the small northern European country of Estonia had all its online infrastructures attacked for weeks to deadly effect. Government agencies, banks and media outlets were disabled. Motivation for the attack may have come from the moving of a statue of Stalin from the capital Tallinn to the outskirts or from Russia's desire for revenge on Estonia for breaking away politically (Estonia took many of the secrets of the Soviet space programme with it as most of the computer programmers were Estonian). However, although the hackers had Russian IP addresses, it was impossible to prove that Russia was responsible because, as mentioned above, cyber hackers' IP addresses can be easily obscured.

In May 2017 an attack, thought to be from North Korea, known as the WannaCry ransomware attack, was unleashed on 150 countries. The Trojan virus disrupted vital information systems from railways to banks and demanded users pay a ransom to restore their data.

According to the UK's Ministry of Defence (MoD), the cost of cyberattacks in 2018 reached roughly US$ 2.1 trillion and this is set to rise by 15% year on year. The major risk according to the MoD is that cyberattacks can disable or shut down industrial facilities and public services.[33]

SME companies

Cyberattacks are usually associated with large companies and the large corporates are those most written about in relation to such attacks; cyber solutions and insurance cover focus on the bigger sized firms. Yet, it is the SME sector that often needs cover the most because in the supply chain they are the weakest link.

Japan, being a country of very large corporations (*shogo shosha*) with large trading arms (*keiretsu*) and dependent on many smaller companies for manufactured parts, is particularly prone to cyberattacks that involve IP theft through the SME supply chains.

On 2 July 2019, the Japanese *Nikkei* newspaper warned that cyberattacks against SME supply chains can have dire consequences because only 4% of SMEs in Japan have countermeasures against cyberattack. This means that cyber assailants can easily steal the IP blueprints of big car manufacturers through attack of the smaller subsidiary SMEs. The Ministry of Economy, Trade and Industry (METI) and other governmental agencies are concerned that this weakness against the cyberattack on the supply chain of SMEs will weaken overall cyber preparedness.[34] SME sectors as a whole need to be analysed within the framework of their special vulnerabilities in terms of being attacked directly as they are seen as both repositories of innovative IP and because they are part of extensive supply chains SMEs are viewed as easy and indirect conduits for stealing IP from larger corporates.

Maritime sector

Other than digitised power grids we also assess the whole maritime world from navies to commercial shipping. Navies constitute the military might of national self-defence while commercial shipping underpins the strength of global trade so integral to economic success of nations. Cyber risk and attack were not taken that seriously in the maritime sector until recently when cyberattack vulnerabilities were becoming increasingly exposed in navies of the world that experienced attacks on GPS navigational systems whether in the straits of Malacca or by Somali pirates in the Horn of Africa. This is changing however, especially with a new report from a government watchdog that stated that the US Department of Transportation's Maritime Administration was showing signs of cyber-vulnerability to 'basic hacker techniques'.[35]

Cyber risk and attack within these sectors have increased so acutely that cybersecurity systems have now become as integral a framework for a ship's safety as structure and machinery according to the Chairman of the International Association of Classification Societies (IACS). The IACS has in fact published numerous recommendations that explain how the shipping industry can make their fleets more resilient against cyberattack and there are further recommendations to come. Cybercriminals until recently have been more intent on searching for their ill-gotten gains by concentrating on banking and finance sectors.[36] Yet, unaccounted for electronic interference such as that recently experienced around the Suez Canal approaches and cyberattacks on navies of the world by local hackers in different ports are a foretaste of how the commercial shipping industry is being targeted. This is placing the onus on commercial shipping to improve their cyber defences more rapidly.

Navies of the world have already risen to the challenge by spending as much on cyber defence as they do on weaponry and ship structures. Navies have a particular vulnerability in relation to IP as the *Weaponry Report: Cyber Security* notes that defence systems are protected by various aspects of IPR.[37] The United States Coast Guard (USCG) has recently issued an alert concerning marine safety in relation to cyberattacks in the form of a cyber malware incident on a deep-draft vessel that impacted its shipboard network. This incident was so serious that it prompted the USCG to request that cyber assessments with regards to cyber vulnerabilities be carried out on all related vessels by vessel and facility owners and operators.[38]

Internet of Things

The Internet of Things (IoT) is defined in my book *Managing Cyber Risk in the Financial Sector* (2016: 15) as the interconnectiveness of all systems through the internet. This affects cyber risk and attack in a more comprehensive manner and also affects the insurance value chain in a similar manner to the aforementioned way SMEs act as a conduit for cyber risk and attack as part of a supply chain for larger companies.

The rapid growth in IoT breaches of cybersecurity is so prevalent that a UK government report in 2018 proposed that IoT training to prevent and deal with cyberattack from individual or state-sponsored actors become part of training for all engineers who work with connected devices. This would include plumbers and gas engineers. The Home Office also proposed investing £5million to train police forces in cybersecurity measures, especially to protect SME companies and individuals. In 2018 only 30% of police forces met the minimum cybercrime capability. Amber Rudd, the Home Secretary, at this time noted that the National Cyber Security Centre (NCSC) had responded to 49 incidents associated with Russian cybergroups with some having hundreds of potential victims.[39] This will be explored in subsequent chapters as indirect entry paths for cyberattack to occur is not made clear in much of the literature, especially in relation to IoT.

Data breaches

Data breaches through IoT or otherwise are being taken very seriously by both governments and companies through regulations and fines. Personal data being breached by hackers who then pass it on for use by fraudsters has been increasing rapidly and making companies realise that it is their responsibility to ensure personal data entrusted to them is not breached in any manner. The recent cases of British Airways and Marriott Hotels are a case in point. The Global Data Protection Regulation (GDPR) was introduced on 25 May 2018 in the EU jurisdiction. British Airways was fined more than £183 million by the Information Commissioner's Office for the breach of a wide range of personal data of half a million of their customers. This seems to be a very large fine but Darren Wray, CEO of Fifth Step a cyber resiliency consultancy, noted that the EU regulator could have fined British Airways up to 4% of their annual revenue, instead of 1.5%, which would have added £300 million to the total fine.[40] British Airways was criticised by the Information Commissioner's Office for not even ensuring basic customer data protection such as rudimentary encryption. The Marriott international hotel chain has been fined £123 million for their 2018 data breach of personal customer information under GDPR and intends to fight it.[41]

Throughout the EU in 2018 there were 206,326 cases of cyberattacks involving data breaches with 52% now closed, 47% ongoing and 1% appealed.[42] Not all firms have integrated GDPR practices into their businesses as yet and for SME companies it is costly, if not financially impossible, to hire a data protection officer.

IP can be seen as both personal and company owned depending on whether it is a sole inventor, single company or patent pool invention.

How will legislation evolve to cover breaches of IP and who will be deemed responsible for such breaches? Will the defence departments of governments be seen as responsible when IP concerning defence plans is breached? IP is much more complicated when theft takes place as the implications are much wider, affecting individuals, companies and governments including infrastructure, defence, education and so forth. The complications of IP, especially through the IoT, not only make it more difficult to protect but also to insure.

The extent and variation of cyberattack is expanding at such a rapid rate that insurers protecting companies both large and small and across all sectors are not able to update their cyber products rapidly enough and are even unsure what are the best policies to offer. In, for example, industries such the maritime sector, the data upon which experience is based to formulate policy cover are not extensive enough. Many of the cyber risk insurance products focus on BI, which is inadequate for the maritime sector as it has to deal with damage resulting from to the loss of vessels' IP data through theft and GPS navigational attacks. The most difficult problem in creating a comprehensive insurance policy for the maritime sector surrounds exclusion, which also exemplifies the heart of the matter surrounding the management of cyber risk/attack explored in this book. This is how we define whether a cyberattack is a result of war or crime. Is a terrorist derived cyberattack an act of war or is it basically a crime when it involves, for example, hacking into a vessel's navigational system to change the course of a ship to land where it can be robbed of its content to fund terrorist activities? The theft of data, IP, or locking companies or public services out from their data such as the WannaCry ransomware attack did can be considered both an act of war and a crime. Is the physical destruction of infrastructure through cyberattack an act of war or a crime? The overlap between the two needs to be explored and definitions/analysis expanded, which we do in subsequent chapters.

Notes

1 A debate covered in my last few books such as *Managing Cyber Risk in the Financial Sector: Lessons from Asia, Europe and USA*, Abingdon: Routledge, 2016.

2 'Fractured system needs urgent fix', Daniel Thomas, *Patents*, *The Times* (18 December 2018).

3 'Predators of the internet who do as they please' Jonathan Taplin, *The Times* (6 May 2017).

4 'Web inventor in battle to avert a digital dystopia', Mark Bridge, *The Times* (25 November 2019).

5 'Pompeo attacks China and warns Britain over Huawei security risks' Stephen Castle, *New York Times* (9 May 2019).

6 PwC Japan, Economic Crime and Fraud Survey 2018. See www.pwc.com/jp/ja/knowledge/thoughtleadership/economic-crime-survey2018.html

7 Ibid.

8 'Insurance industry must learn from global markets to meet challenge of huge rise in cyber-risk', James Brewer, *AllAboutShipping* (18 March 2016).

9 'IUA publishes cyber exclusion clauses', Scott Farley, Communications Director, *IUA Press Release* (5 June 2019).

10 *Creating Value for the Cyber Risk Agenda* (10 June 2019). See https://aon.io/2KwPoaQ

11 See, for example, 'BA staff warn over data vulnerabilities', Josh Spero, *Financial Times* (25 March 2019).

12 'Two from China are charged in Anthem breach', Nicole Perlroth, *New York Times* (9 May 2019).

13 'FBI wishes it had acted quicker as China stole intellectual property', Daphne Psaledakis, *Reuters* (19 November 2019).

14 'Without naming Huawei, E.U. warns against 5G firms from hostile powers', *Advisen Cyber News, Digest Edition* (15 October 2019).

15 'The church going patriot who spied for China', Tara McElvey, Kevin Mallor, *New York Times* (15 January 2019).

16 'Bank of Lithuania: cybercrimes are the greatest risk to the domestic financial system', *The Baltic Course* (13 July 2018). See www.baltic-course.com/eng/finances/?doc=141487

17 'Lithuania ranks 4th in global cybersecurity index', *The Baltic Course* (1 April 2019). See www.baltic-course.com/eng/good_for_business/?doc=148303

18 'Britain is "at war every day" due to constant cyber attacks, Chief of the Defence Staff says', Dominic Nicholls, *The Telegraph* (29 September 2019).

19 'Cyber "war" demands new redefined borders reinsure says', Erin Ayers, *Advisen Cyber News, Digest Edition* (25 July 2019).

20 'Army trains keyboard warriors for digital war', Dominic Nicholls, *The Daily Telegraph* (1 August 2019).

21 See 'China hacked a Navy contractor and secured a trove of highly sensitive data on submarine warfare', Ellen Nakashima and Paul Sonne, *Washington Post* (8 June 2018). See www.washingtonpost.com/world/national-security/china-hacked-a-navy-contractor-and-secured-a-trove-of-highly-sensitive-data-on-submarine-warfare/2018/06/08/6cc396fa-68e6-11e8-bea7-c8eb28bc52b1_story.html?utm_term=.3464eeb0538a)

22 'Boom time for the cyberdogs of war', Ben MacIntyre, *The Times* (17 February 2018).

23 'White House is pressing for additional options including cyberattacks on Iran', Julian E. Barnes, Eric Schmitt and Thomas Gibbons-Neff, *New York Times* (23 June 2019).

24 'UK could consider joining Trump in war on Iran says Hunt as potential PM vows to consider support on "case-by-case" basis', Michael Blackely and James Tapsfield, *Daily Mail Online* (24 June 2019).

25 'Oil and gas industry "open to cyberattack"', *The Times* (18 August 2018).
26 'In aviation cybersecurity awareness has been met by greater challenges', Erin Ayers, *Advisen Cyber News* (16 December 2019).
27 'Global shipping industry hears a "wake-up call" on cyber risk: Allianz', Erin Ayers, *Advisen Cyber News Online Digest* (7 June 2019).
28 'Labcorp discloses data breach affecting 7.7 million customers', *Advisen Cyber News Online Digest* (6 June 2019).
29 'Huawei is said to demand patent fees from Verizon', Paul Mozur and Edmund Lee, *New York Times* (12 June 2019).
30 'Chinese cyberattack hits Telegram app used by protestors', Paul Mozur and Alexandra Stevenson, *New York Times* (14 June 2019).
31 See P. Lis and J. Mendel (2019) 'Cyberattacks on critical infrastructure: an economic perspective'. *Economics and Business Review, 5(19)*(2), 24–47, https://doi.org/10.18559/ebr.2019.2.2. J. Mendel (2018) 'The economic perspective on smart grid cyber security'. Unpublished doctoral dissertation completed in the Department of Economics, the University of Poznan, Poland.
32 'U.S. escalates online attacks on Russia's power grid', David E. Sanger and Nicole Perlroth, *New York Times* (15 June 2019).
33 'New targets in worldwide cyberwarfare, future of manufacturing', Nafeez Ahmed, *The Times* (19 February 2019, p. 12).
34 'Digital trend – cybersecurity measures in SMEs – thorough preparedness at 4%', Mari Ishibashi, *Nikkei Keizai Shimbun* (2 July 2019).
35 'US maritime agency's cybersecurity found lacking in inspector's report', Erin Ayers, *Advisen Cyber News, Digest Edition* (29 July 2019).
36 See Ruth Taplin (ed.), *Managing Cyber Risk in the Financial Sector: Lessons from Asia, Europe and USA*, Abingdon: Routledge, 2016.
37 'Building resilience, special report: cyber security', Michel Grey, *The Intelligence* (October/November 2018, p. 29).
38 Marine Safety Alert 06-19, *Cyber Incident Exposes Potential Vulnerabilities Onboard Commercial Vessels*, American P&I Club (10 July 2019).
39 'Plumbers recruited to fight cybercrime', Katie Gibbons, *The Times* (12 April 2018).
40 'British Airways fined £183m after cyber breach – but did it get off lightly?' Darren Wray, CEO, Fifth Step Consultancy, press release (9 July 2019).
41 'Marriott, British Airways handed record fines under GDPR', Erin Ayers, *Advisen Cyber News, Digest Edition* (11 July 2019).
42 'British Airways fined £183m after cyber breach – but did it get off lightly?' Darren Wray, CEO, Fifth Step Consultancy, press release (9 July 2019).

2 IP theft and cyberwarfare

Where and by whom?

The majority of technological advances are created and funded by a state's military whether in the US, China, Britain or Russia. Therefore, it should be no surprise that a good deal of IP theft is related to the development of cyberwarfare. The object of the exercise is to gain an intelligence advantage in gathering data and blueprints of new defence strategies. Cyberattacks are being used to penetrate the defences of the relatively new arena of cyberwarfare that is led by generals.[1]

Such technological advances are secondly furthered by industry through research and design (R&D), often through shared patent pools. The aim is to outperform rival companies and dominate trade and manufacturing. IP theft is rife to gain market dominance.

The exploitation of such technological advances and IP is often by geopolitical forces that wish to undermine political rivals in other geographical locations or those considered domestic political enemies including terrorists.

Finally, there is the pure criminal element of greed for personal advantage, personal inadequacy or malice that drives cyberattack and IP theft. The latter may not even be the main target but is part of the process of stealing something valuable for pecuniary gain.

To complicate matters even further there exist state-sponsored hacking groups that target a variety of industries covered in this book for not only intelligence or patent gains, but also for pecuniary purposes. A new report from Fireeye notes that such dual cyberattack activity is both new and increasing in scope.[2]

A recent example of this tendency are the state-sponsored Chinese hackers who as a sideline use their hacking skills to carry out cyberattacks on cryptocurrency providers and gaming companies for their own personal gain. One group of Chinese hackers called Advanced Persistence Threat 41 (APT41) are the most effective of such state-sponsored cyberespionage hackers. Since its inception in 2012, APT41 has carried out cyberattacks on a variety of organisations in 14 countries including the US, UK Europe and Asia. The main focus has been breaching the data systems of those companies in the healthcare, news, education, high-tech, telecommunications, travel and video gaming sectors. APT41 and its sister organisation APT10, which specialises in attacks on utility companies such as the three in the US in July 2019, demonstrate that cyberwarfare based on geo-political rivalry, IP theft and personal greed can all meld into one in the cases of large cyberattacks.

APT41 has allegedly carried out IP theft on a large scale against pharmaceutical companies in the US and Europe, while gathering intelligence for the Chinese state on pro-democracy demonstrations in Hong Kong, which have been increasing recently. Financially motivated cyberattacks for individual gain have until 2014 been almost non-existent for Chinese state-sponsored hackers who are usually well-funded by the state. However, in 2014, video gaming companies became a target by these groups for personal pecuniary gain. Chinese state-sponsored hackers breached the video gaming systems such as *Fifa Online*, which has millions of followers. This can bring in millions of dollars in revenue to satiate individual greed for these hackers who also advertise their willingness to hack on a hire basis.

The current trade war initiated by President Trump in relation to tariff rises has been linked to a great extent to IP theft by the Chinese state from the US government and companies.[3]

Even cyberespionage tools used by the US National Security Agency (NSA) have been stolen by a Chinese hacking group linked to the Beijing-based Ministry of State Security. APT3, also known as Buckeye or Gothic Panda, has been stealing hacking codes used by the NSA to infiltrate networks such as the disabling of the Iranian nuclear programme in 2010. The problem for the NSA is that such attacks leave traces of malware codes, which can be lifted and reconstructed to expose NSA tools. APT3 is based in Mainland China's south-eastern Guangdong Province and has been active since at least 2009. However, in 2019, as mentioned in Chapter 1 of this book, the US Justice Department charged and later prosecuted two members of APT3 for stealing information over a six-year period, including IP from Trimble, a satellite software firm, Siemens and Moody's Analytics, the financial services company. Chinese hackers have targeted many US sectors such as NASA space technology, aeronautics, defence, oil and gas companies and the biotechnology sector mainly to steal IP and private information. APT3's theft of NSA tools was the first known instance of a foreign-based state group stealing codes through an active hack.

This led Christopher Wray, the Director of the FBI, to state that Chinese state-sponsored hacking groups as the 'most active perpetrators of economic espionage against us' and '[n]o country poses a broader, more severe and long-term threat to our nation's economy and cyber-infrastructure than China'.

The number of APT groups and the number of members of those APT groups keep increasing. Their cyberattacks on the US are expanding such as APT40's attacks on research universities with ties to the US Navy.[4]

Counter accusations and IP theft

Another example of how allegations and actual cases of IP theft are integrally linked to geo-political cyber and economic warfare are the recent counter accusations of the Chinese telecommunications company Huawei against the US and a case of patent theft by the Chinese company.

Huawei has made accusations against the US government stating that the FBI had visited Huawei's employees' homes trying to force them to spy for the US and had committed cyberattacks on the internal workings of Huawei. This was alleged without any evidence but within the context of the US government trying to block and persuade users and US telecommunications companies not to use Huawei equipment and not to sell them parts because they are seen as a security risk. Such action included requesting Qualcomm not to sell its microchips and Google its smartphone software. The US Commerce Department underscored this action by placing Huawei on a blacklist for exporting companies. The NSA already in 2010 had begun investigating and actually intruding into their servers to find out how Huawei operated as they were suspicious of their intent as a security threat.

That has triggered the latest accusations by the US government connected to a report in the *Wall Street Journal* that Huawei had stolen patents from a Portuguese multimedia designer. Huawei noted in its statement that its representatives had met with Mr Rui Olivera in 2014 to discuss using his patented design for a smartphone camera but decided against using it. In 2017 Huawei had developed its own smartphone camera, which in 2018 Mr Olivera claimed was a violation of his US-based patents and he threatened to expose Huawei in the news media if they did not compensate him for this infringement. Huawei in turn filed in the US courts a request stating that they did not infringe Mr Olivera's patent, which the US officials are still investigating.[5]

Cyberattack to fund IP theft for WMD

North Korea is a country that is using cyberattack to raise funds for weapons of mass destruction (WMD). This is a case of cyber being used to produce a possible tangible, physical war on its neighbours or for domestic use to control its population. The UN Security Council made public a report that more than US$ 2 billion have been stolen by North Korean hackers to fund nuclear and non-nuclear ballistic missile programmes. The stolen monies have been obtained from the financial institutions such as banks that still have dealings with North Korea despite sanctions being in place, which allows North Koreans to hack these countries more easily than countries that have no connections at all adhering to sanctions. North Korean hackers target in particular cryptocurrencies such as Bitcoin as they are not subject to individual country regulation and scrutiny. This means that the North Korean government can obtain through cyberattack vast amounts of revenue that cannot be easily traced to source and steal IP related to WMD development from other countries. The bulk of these monies the UN report found were not used to develop North Korea and enrich its citizens but to keep Kim Jong-un in luxury and his military up-to-date with latest military technology for weaponry that can be used for WMD.[6]

Russian cyberwarfare and IP theft

There are numerous examples of issues of cyberwarfare, geo-political/military rivalry and personal monetary gain driving the numerous cyberattacks that emanate from Russia, central and Eastern European countries.

In a curious case in Bulgaria, which highlights the difficulty of tracing both the culprits and motives for cyberattacks, a young Bulgarian was accused of a major cyberattack. A 20-year-old from Bulgaria's second largest city Plovdiv has been accused of carrying out the largest cyberattack in Bulgaria involving the theft of personal data from every working adult in the country from the National Revenue Agency. The young man denied all charges and both security experts and Western intelligence did not subscribe to this account of events.

The timing of the public release of all the hacked data from a Russian IP address when Bulgaria was strengthening its relationship with NATO by purchasing eight F-16 fighter jets made the accusations against the young Bulgarian seem ludicrous. This was especially the case as the F-16 purchase was a plan by the Americans to bring Bulgaria's fighting forces on a par with NATO, replacing ageing Soviet jets.

However, this breach was carried out with one of the most basic tools used by hackers, an SQL (structured query language) injection in which the cyberattacker uses a login page to insert a malicious code that allows access to data. What this cyberattack points to is the lack of preparedness by the Bulgarian government to be cyber ready and even put in place basic countermeasures to combat such hacking.

'While an enthusiastic member of NATO, Bulgaria has weak and porous cyberdefenses – probably the worst in the alliance,' said Admiral James G. Stavridis, a four-star former NATO military commander. He continued: 'Significant cybercriminal activity, including some sponsored by the Russian state, is rife', and '[a]ny "shield wall" is only as strong as the weakest barrier, and the linkages into NATO infrastructure via Bulgaria during exercises and deployments there are concerning'.[7] In other words, cyberattacks that are successful are based on finding the weakest links to enter a system that can further cyberwarfare, IP theft and geo-political ends.

Bulgaria's geo-political importance to NATO and Russia is marked as it lies between the Visegrád countries of Eastern Europe such as Poland, the Czech Republic, Hungary and Slovakia.

Geo-political importance of Visegrád countries for cyberwarfare

An early example of cyberwarfare that was described as such by Estonian officials occurred already in 2007. The cyberattack emanating from Russia shut down the government, media and banking systems. This extreme cyberattack followed the Estonian decision to remove a war memorial from the Soviet era when Estonia was used by Russians as the cyber experts to drive their space programme. Russian leaders initially denounced the war memorial removal and stoked antagonisms between ethnic Russians and Estonians, which became violent and deadly.

Such cyberwarfare tactics have not abated but intensified mainly via social media throughout the world. This was seen in the 2016 elections in the US when the social media was inundated with conspiracy theories and the demonising of presidential hopeful Hillary Clinton. The FBI is currently concerned that the 2020 elections will once more be interfered with by Russian hackers.[8]

Geo-political cyberwarfare attacks are becoming increasingly sophisticated and, consequently, more difficult to locate, isolate and combat. Often it is experts who expose Russian cyberattacks that are becoming the target of such political cyberwarfare. ProtonMail and its experts of the European Values Think-Tank were targeted in late July 2019 by what their CEO described as 'the most sophisticated [he has] ever encountered'. The phishing cyberattack, according to the investigative group Bellingcat, targeted those analysing Russian geo-political strategies. Those targeted included BBC/*Guardian* investigative journalists, Bellingcat researchers, and academics who are focused on Kremlin foreign policy. Due to the complexity of this cyberattack it was difficult to pinpoint the perpetrator but Bellingcat investigators were quite sure it was the Russian GRU (military secret service).

Clues to the Russian cyberattack

A number of clues made the Russian GRU the likely suspected perpetrator:

- The source codes that were used on the phishing sites pointed to a state actor rather than any individual hacker.
- The planning time of the cyberattack was a year, which is indicative of state actors who have the resources to devote such a long period of time and human resources.

Bellingcat was able to reconstruct a good deal of the malicious code that modified the ProtonMail image creating a fake one which began being worked on 8 March 2018, a year before the massive cyberattack.

- Another clue to the origins of the phishing cyberattack was that a test site linked to the final attack was discovered by Marcus Neis, the Threat Intel Manager at Swisscom who discovered an overlapping fingerprint on his company's site with one of the phishing sites.

Jakub Janda, Executive Director of European Values Think-Tank, stated:

> The fact that our analysts are targets of such sophisticated operations alongside the elite of Western investigators of Russian hostilities only confirms to us that we have targets on our backs. That is the price you pay for exposing hostile activities by the Russian dictatorship also in our Central and Eastern European region. None of our critical data were compromised during this incident. We would like to thank to security institutions of democratic countries who are helping to protect people like us and many others.[9]

Eastern European foreign ministries attacked

Foreign ministries are not exempt from cyberattacks, especially those that are part of NATO and therefore hold a close relationship to the US military. The Czech Ministry of Foreign Affairs experiences cyberattacks weekly. In January 2017 the cyberattacks increased dramatically and followed the same pattern as those that were targeted against the Democratic National Committee (DNC) in the US. The Czech Foreign Minister stated there were no major breaches of confidential information and did not mention the state actor that may have been responsible. However, a government source reported that it was most likely Russia. It has been speculated that the major cyberattack could have been carried out by the Russian Cyber Army as vengeance for the Czech Republic's close relationship with NATO and the EU.[10]

Iran as a source of geo-political cyberattacks

Iran, along with Russia, has been initiating cyberattacks for geo-political reasons. In early October 2019 Microsoft stated that 2,700 hacking attempts were made in relation to a presidential campaign, American journalists who were covering Iran-US relations and US government departments. Unsophisticated methods were used to find out passwords to access victims' accounts through finding out information about the victims initially. Iran is following the example Russia set of trying to interfere through geo-political cyberattacks. In July 2019 Tim Burt, Corporate Vice President of Microsoft, said that the majority of geo-political cyberattacks now emanate from Russia, Iran and North Korea targeting NGOs and think-tanks that work with US political campaigns.[11]

The IoT's growing importance

The Russian model of cyber as an economic and political weapon involves cyberattack in various forms, denial that they are responsible, placing the blame on others, especially proxies, and using cyberwarfare to produce economic, political, social and infrastructural physical damage. Their whole modus operandi relies on stealth, deceit, denial and blaming others. This means they choose cyber mechanisms that are not easy to detect and that are indirect in nature.

Therefore, an increasing use of the IoT, as mentioned in Chapter 1, is taking place. A prime example occurred in April 2019 when Microsoft reported an incident through its Threat Intelligence Center that an IoT cyberattack had been carried out through Voice Over Internet Protocol, a printer and video decoder. The IoT devices provided soft access to a number of locations in the wider corporate network. Two of the three devices had factory security settings while the third had not been updated as yet.

Microsoft noted the cyberattack bore the hallmarks of Russian hackers who are linked to the GRU using a variety of names such as Fancy Bear, APT28 and Strontium. This group of Russian state hackers have been active since 2007 as outlined above but since April 2019 Microsoft noticed that the direction of their cyberattack focus changed to IoT. It is usually thought that hackers target smartphones and computers for easy access to data and information or implanting malicious devices but it is more often that cameras, printers and decoders offer the soft access. The point of access to these devices are default passwords or passwords that are not updated. With the security not updated, the hackers create a beachhead that is their starting point for entering the unprotected corporate networks. Once the hacker has established a firm access to the network, a simple scan of the network for additional insecure devices allows them to move to more high-value accounts offering data and other privileged information. From there, the hackers move from one device to another, all the while mapping the network and communicating with command and control services.

Microsoft has been observing an increase in global activity from the Russian state hackers. Since the initial cyberattack Microsoft has notified 1,400 recipients who have been compromised by APT28 or Fancy Bear. Of those targeted 20% have been think-tanks such as European Values mentioned above, politically affiliated organisations and NGOs. The remainder, which comprises 80% of the cyberattacks, includes, among others, education, technology, engineering, medicine, the military, Olympic organisers, anti-doping agencies and the hospitality industry. In 2018, the FBI took action to disrupt a Fancy Bear campaign named VPNFilter, which targeted network storage devices and routers with malware that had the destructive capacity of 'bricking' devices through deleting firmware and rendering the devices useless. This campaign targeted the Ukraine in particular, which is often the target of Russian state hackers.[12]

As IoT devices rapidly increase and less sophisticated, low-technology devices become the entry point for skilled hackers, in this case Russian state actors, the severity of the cyberattack/cyberwarfare continues. The extent of this cyber risk in relation to IoT was demonstrated when security researchers at Armis found that VxWorks, the operating system that powers all the IoT devices globally, had vulnerabilities in multiple zero-day areas. This disclosure meant that the low-technology devices connected in IoT such as firewalls, medical equipment such as telemedicine platforms, and printers could as described above produce soft access points to corporate networks, which would render multiple layers of security useless.

Microsoft noted that part of the problem is that IoT devices are just interconnected facilitators with little if no management oversight. How many companies hire staff to look after the vulnerabilities of their printers? In fact Microsoft noted that most of their customer IT operations do not know that their simple devices are connected to the internet. Worse, a network analysis showed that the IoT devices are subject to external control and command, which allows ingress from hackers hunting further access points. Microsoft made this disclosure to alert companies to the cyber risks they face especially as the number of IoT devices are far in excess of personal computers (PCs) and mobile phones combined. The sectors particularly vulnerable to cyberattack to be covered in this book will also be assessed in terms of IoT vulnerability as in my previous book on managing cyber risk in the financial sector.[13]

There have been warnings for years from cybercrime experts that even the humble office coffee machine can be a target of cybercriminals because of the ease of entry and also it is cheap for criminals to buy ransomware from dark web sites. In such cases it is even possible to buy one ransomware, get one free and share profits with the people have written the code. Jamie Bartlett, Director of the Centre for Analysis of Social Media at Demos, noted the IoT is so poorly designed that it could in the future become possible to be forced to pay a small ransom in cryptocurrency to obtain coffee from the office coffee machine.[14]

Cryptocurrencies – another cyber risk

Cryptocurrencies present another opportunity for cyber hackers whether state actors or individuals to flourish. The seemingly innocent alternative currency system provides cover for a whole host of cybercriminals.

A prime example is the North Korean state actors who use increasingly sophisticated means to procure finance through cyberattack/cyberwarfare. A recent UN report outlined the ways in which North Korean state-backed cyber hackers have stolen at least US$ 2 billion from financial institutions and in cryptocurrencies. Such monies, which are either regulated by global nation-states or unregulated speculators in the case of cryptocurrencies, are used to build WMD and missiles to threaten their enemies around the world except for its backer Mainland China. The UN report is 33 pages in length with 192 annexes that chronicle at least 35 examples of North Korean state actors stealing monies from financial institutions and cryptocurrencies. This is in addition to stealing IP blueprints from advanced missile-producing countries globally. Cryptocurrencies are preferred targets for cyber theft because according to the UN report they are harder to trace, not being subject to regulation and oversight by different countries' central banking systems. Such illegal transfer of funds from countries outside North Korea is facilitated by 30 overseas North Korean banking outlets.[15]

The advance in cryptocurrency use is facing many hurdles in the case of Mark Zuckerberg, CEO of Facebook, trying to launch a new cryptocurrency entitled Libra. This move has been met with scepticism given the criticisms of how Facebook was used by the Russians to bias the 2016 American presidential election towards Donald Trump through social media.

There have been moves by countries that have rogue dictators as leaders and small island countries to also issue cryptocurrencies, which would boost their economies and also allow dictatorships such as North Korea to launder money from ill-gotten gains. Venezuela has tried unsuccessfully to launch a sovereign cryptocurrency, the petro but it has failed. The government of the small Marshall Islands has launched in 2018 a SOV Development Fund to create a cryptocurrency named the SOV. The government has passed a bill in the legislature to support the SOV as it would raise much-needed revenue for the islanders who have suffered from a US crackdown on money laundering, which has raised compliance fees and most banks no longer wish to operate in the Marshall Islands. With the SOV the Marshall Islands can send their own money directly without using the global banking system. The problem is when recipients try to convert the SOV into dollars or other local currencies. In addition the International Monetary Fund and the US Treasury have raised concerns that such SOV-based revenue building could come at a high cost to the Marshall Islands' reputation and money-laundering risks. The Marshall Islands government in turn has argued that the SOV will be tamper proof and allow for lower-cost compliance to be instituted.[16]

Cryptocurrencies are becoming less attractive in mainstream markets because of the risks they pose and their use by cybercriminals especially increasingly in relation to ransomware attacks. UK marine engineering firm London Offshore Consultants (LOC) were hacked by a group called Maze who claimed they stole 300GB of data and leaked some of this online to pressure LOC to pay the ransom to unlock their frozen computers. Early in December 2019 the FBI had warned that Maze ransomware attacks had been identified since November of that year, often posing as US government agencies, stealing data, then encrypting it to be able to extort victims further. One of the multiple methods Maze used was their own creation of a malicious, fake cryptocurrency site in addition to malspam to impersonate government agencies.[17]

Supply-chain cyberattack entry

Another route for obtaining data, IP theft and the implantation of malware that has not been given adequate attention by companies leading to indirect breaches from both individuals and state actors is through supply chains. Most companies large and small, as well as government agencies, rely on some form of supply chain, which is required for both products and services. In fact, the larger the company the more it relies on supply chains. A recent example involves two hotel chains, one with 107 hotels in 14 countries and the other with 73 hotels in 14 countries worldwide. A Magecard skimming campaign compromised the hotels' mobile websites through a third-party supply chain. Trend Micro researchers found that hackers had targeted Roomleader based in Barcelona implanting a malicious Javascript. Roomleader offers digital marketing and website development services assisting hospitality companies with their booking functions through a library module named 'viewedhotels', which serves to save viewed hotel information in guests' browser cookies. In line with the usual Magecart attacks the skimmer was designed to glean information and data concerning guests' contact details such as e-mail addresses, credit card details and room preferences. In this case the skimmer card was constructed to only target mobile website use and not those who had utilised their PCs. Desktop users in fact were sent booking information using the normal Javascript. Joseph Chen, the fraud researcher at Trend Micro, suggested that mobile websites were targeted because they were not protected by the usual PC security software and were easier to enter while escaping detection. The hackers replaced the hotel payment forms with their own slightly different version but translated them into eight different languages like the original payment forms to help avoid detection. Additionally, many hotels do not ask guests for their Card Verification Code (CVC) doing so when the guests arrive. In their replacement payment forms they were sure to request guest CVC security codes.[18]

A recent survey by Microsoft and insurance company Marsh, significant companies in both producing computers and insuring their use, reported that company leaders have become even more concerned about the rapid increase in cyberattack. Yet, these business leaders and executives are even less confident than they were in dealing with such cyber risks.[19]

Notes

1 'Good for Google, bad for America', Peter Thiel, *New York Times* (1 August 2019).
2 'Cybercrime and espionage go hand in hand as groups target healthcare and video game world', Erin Ayers, *Advisen Cyber News, Digest Edition* (8 August 2019).
3 'Beijing hackers moonlight for cash', Boer Deng, *The Times* (9 August 2019).
4 'Chinese hackers "turned" US spy tools on West', Boer Deng, *The Times* (8 May 2019).
5 'Huawei says without evidence that U.S. pressured its employees', Raymond Zhong, *New York Times* (3 September 2019).
6 'North Korea "stole $2bn for weapons via cyber-attacks"', *BBC News Online* (7 August 2019). See www.bbc.co.uk/news/world-asia-49259302
7 'Russia suspected by some in giant Bulgarian hack', Marc Santora and Eric Schmitt, *New York Times* (14 August 2019).
8 'Episode 13: "The Blueprint"', Producer/Director John Marks, *New York Times* (6 September 2019).

9 'European Values Think-Tank among 30 Russian watchers targeted by the most sophisticated cyber attack ever done on ProtonMail, probably by the GRU', press release, *European Values* (14 August 2019). N.B. Technical details of this cyberattack were made public by Bellingcat.
10 'Cyber attack on Ministry of Foreign Affairs', Naveen Goud, *Cybersecurity Insiders*. See www.cybersecurity-insiders.com/cyber-attack-on-czech-ministry-of-foreign-affairs/
11 'Iranian hackers targeted presidential campaign, Microsoft says', Nicole Perlroth, *New York Times* (4 October 2019).
12 'Microsoft warns Russian hackers can breach secure networks through simple IoT devices', Zak Doffman, *Forbes* (5 August 2019). 'Russian hacks are infiltrating companies through the office printer', *MIT Technology Review Computing* (5 September 2019).
13 'Microsoft warns Russian hackers can breach secure networks through simple IoT devices', Zak Doffman, *Forbes* (5 August 2019). Ruth Taplin (ed.), *Managing Cyber Risk in the Financial Sector: Lessons from Japan, Europe and the USA*, Abingdon: Routledge, 2016.
14 'It's time to wake up and smell coffee on cybercrime', Alexandra Frean, *The Times* (16 November 2017).
15 'North Korea skirted U.N. sanctions and earned US$ 2 billion using cyberattacks, a new U.N. Report says', Pamela Falk, *CBS News* (6 August 2019).
16 'North Korea stole 2 billion hacking financial bodies – UN report', *MIT Technology Review Computing* (5 September 2019).
17 'London Offshore Consultants suffers ransomware attack', Sam Chambers, *Splash 24/7* (31 January 2020).
18 'Hotel websites infected with skimmer via supply chain attack', Bradley Barth, *SC Media* (18 September 2019).
19 'Businesses more concerned about cyber risks, but less confident in ability to manage it: Marsh', Erin Ayers, *Advisen Cyber News, Digest Edition* (19 September 2019).

3 Japan

Japan is a country that holds many contradictions in relation to dealing with managing cyber risk including IP theft and issues of cyberwarfare, which will be explored in this chapter. It is not widely known that IP theft is the most frequent form of cyberattack and cyber theft. Japan has been and is still an innovative country producing in the past the blue-emitting diode invented by Nakamura Shuji and currently being a leader in developing medical devices for the elderly. These all create IP especially in terms of patents. Japanese companies, because of the high costs of R&D, work together with other parts of their companies or external companies in terms of patent pools. This means resources and expenses are shared as well as the results of the patent that ensues. The Japanese government is one of the most methodical in the world in terms of preparing for cyberattack. This can be seen in the current preparations against cyberattack organised for the 2021 Olympics in Japan. Plans are meticulously prepared in the smallest detail with hundreds of supporting diagrams and many committees. In Japan plans are coordinated from the bottom up to the top and then top down. Such preparations are often compared to preparing the roots of trees properly before the tress are moved in early winter. This is a decision-making process called *nemawashi.*[1]

Such cyber readiness is then often undermined by the lack of computer literacy. When visiting many companies over the years, it never ceases to amaze me how many Japanese employees are computer illiterate all across business activity whether in the hospitality industry or medical services. Perhaps even more astounding is the minister in charge of cybersecurity that includes stopping cyberattacks through computers or mobile phones for the 2021 Tokyo Olympics, Mr Sakurada Yoshitaka, has never in his life used a computer and had little idea what to with a USB stick. He said since he was 25 years old and started his career, he always delegated any computer-related tasks to his staff and secretaries.[2]

Perhaps it is the Japanese concepts of *tatamae* and *honne* that enable Japanese with such contradictions: *tatamae* refers to how things should be while *honne* means how things actually are in reality.[3] This means that any understanding of cyberattack in terms of IP theft, cyberwarfare, cyber risk and management requires an analysis rooted within this contradictory framework.

To understand the strengths and weaknesses of cyberattacks in terms of IP theft and cyberwarfare on business it is essential to understand the organisation of the large corporate conglomerates (the *shogo shosha*) and their trading arms (the *keiretsu*) vis-à-vis their SME suppliers in the supply chain. This is because supply-chain SMEs are often the weakest link in which hackers, either individuals or state actors, use as a softer access point to carry out a cyberattack on the larger corporate organisation.

Shogo shosha and SMEs

Japanese companies originate from the traditional *zaibatsu*, which consisted of family-owned conglomerates such as the oldest *zaibatsu* Mitsui, which became a huge network of cross-shareholding firms. The nature of the cross-shareholdings were very secretive and only very trusted outsiders were let into the family dealings. Many subordinate companies such as *keiretsu* or trading arms were formed that have different names from the parent companies but are an integral part of them through cross-shareholding.

Zaibatsu were banned by the American administrators after the Second World War and were replaced by *shogo shosha* that followed the same pattern of the *zaibatsu* but without ostensibly the family-centred control. The *shogo shosha* has at its centre, the financial heart, a bank. The Mitsui bank, for example, or the Mitsubishi bank lends finance and holds remittances from the other related company arms. This octopus-like structure that is all essentially inter-related, makes it very difficult for intruders in the form of cyberattackers to penetrate. Loyalty to the conglomerate organisation is at a premium and any that would try to undermine the tightly knit structure of the related companies would be socially ostracised and left in a very unpleasant position of extreme isolation.

Group and hierarchal decision-making

The emphasis on harmony and the group has its roots traditionally in wet rice agriculture where all members of the group are consulted with group consensus and harmony taking precedence over any other form of group organisation. Group consensus is both formal and informal but both solidify interpersonal relations. In companies, relationships between employers and employees are bound up with obligatory polite ritual that consistently emphasises rank and formality. Yet, the management by consensus from the top-down/bottom-up approach is linked to ideas of groupism with informality linked to ideas of egalitarianism. Therefore, once employers and employees are out of their offices, informal socialising takes place with often the most important socialising taking place.

Control in Japanese companies is delegated down throughout all levels of management not just by senior officials. Delegation operates through the entire ranking system from *shacho* (president), *juyaki* (director), *bucho* (department head) and *kacho* (section head). The *hira-shain* (ordinary worker) is mainly involved in decision-making through quality circles and the suggestion system or in other limited ways that have direct implications for their jobs.

The delegations throughout the company are real and not just token titles of delegation. Employees throughout the company, and even operators of their own machines, are actually given functional power over their environment and over the decisions needed to be made with regard to their working situations, but only to improve productivity. A department or section head can exercise quite a high degree of power and control over his own particular job requirements. This may be related once more to the basic cultural assumptions of egalitarianism and groupism with people trusting each other to govern, because they are expected to take responsibility. Social responsibility and the social pressure of potentially losing face obviates the need to be constantly constrained by laws. People are to be trusted by their superiors because of their social control function of obligation and consensus and therefore are empowered to be responsible for their own particular functions in the company, in society or in the family. The heavy emphasis on social consensus ensures that social control will compel people to behave in a socially responsible manner. Unwritten social 'law' governs the behaviour of the Japanese, even in circumstances such as terms of employment, in which a legal contract would be demanded by employees of a company in the West. Therefore, with such demands on loyalty, the binding constraints of obligation and being an integral part of the company decision-making, the possibilities for hackers to break into the closed ranks of Japanese company employees or for an internal employee to cyberattack another member of the same company is slim indeed.[4]

Supply-chain cyber weaknesses

Supply chains are becoming more advanced in Japan having increased dealings with companies in other countries. It was found in a recent survey by the Osaka Chamber of Commerce that only 4% of SMEs in Japan have implemented information security measures according to government guidelines on cyber risk. Osaka has been traditionally a major centre of SMEs supplying *shogo shosha*, having their own trade-union-like organisation that is local to their members. The survey also showed that the majority of the SME companies had digital systems that allowed unauthorised access.

An example of such breaches was an auto parts manufacturer in Tokyo that received a warning from its car maker client that suspect e-mails were received from it which were infected with viruses. This was potentially a very dangerous breach for the client's company by the SME manufacturer as the latter held sensitive information concerning orders in particular. The SME supplier company, as most others, could not afford to hire a bespoke IT manager, so the large client company had the supply company visit its IT company providers to organise effective security measures to resolve the problem.

SMEs under cyberattack

The Osaka Chamber of Commerce, which has had an IT-related department since 1971, selected in September 2018, 30 SME companies to monitor. The survey was assessing external communication with their offices over a three-month timeframe and found that all of them had suspicious e-mails related to a cyberattack. Although all the SMEs monitored were subject to some form of cyberattack, none of them actually understood the full nature of the attack.

There is a growing concern over a potential impact on supply chains due to a delay in implementing information security measures among SMEs. According to this survey by the Osaka Chamber of Commerce, only 4% of SMEs have implemented measures that comply with the guidelines issued by a public body. As supply chains have become more advanced, there is a growing risk of a leak of trade secrets held by major companies through SMEs to foreign countries.

The auto parts manufacturer in Tokyo received a warning from its consignor, a car maker, saying that they had received suspicious e-mails from it. It turned out that this manufacturer's PCs were infected by viruses that then affected the large car maker. The manufacturer had been dealing with important data related to orders coming from the car maker. As this SME did not have anyone in charge of IT, it visited an IT company designated by the car maker to resolve the matter and to set up security measures that hitherto were not present.

Mr Ooshiba of the Security Business Department of Digital Hearts, a software inspection provider in Tokyo, stated in relation to this situation: 'They are aiming to steal the design drawing of cars manufactured by a major car maker by way of SMEs that are poorly prepared against cyberattacks.' No matter how hard major car makers implement countermeasures, important information that is shared with their contractors will be put at risk if these contractors remain vulnerable to cyberattacks.[5]

The above assessment has been supported by another survey by Dell Japan and EMC Japan between 2017–2018 that showed that only 4% of Japanese SMEs had adopted the security measures recommended by the Information-technology Protection Agency (IPA). A study by Dell Japan carried out between December 2018 and December 2019 showed that only 38% of SMEs had one bespoke IT person while 19% were without any specialised IT person. In 2017, the IPA carried out 1,249 interviews with large companies concerning cybersecurity risks linked to supply chains. They found that only 47% had knowledge of the cybersecurity measures of their sub-contractors or consignees with whom they had no direct contact. Outsourcing therefore produced further layers of risk that were difficult for large companies to trace.

The IPA has issued a statement of '10 major threats to the information security business 2019' showing that supply-chain cyber risk now ranks fourth for the first time.

Domestic cyber risk is not necessarily the greatest risk for supply-chain attack. Overseas hackers, whether individuals or state actors, carry out cyberattacks through phishing e-mails to infect supply-chain SMEs that have not adopted rigorous countermeasures.

The situation is such a serious one that a number of public bodies are making an effort to research to find out the extent and nature of the breaches. The Ministry of Economy, Trade and Industry, the IPA, and the aforementioned Digital Hearts will be carrying out a survey on cyberattack damage to 100–200 companies in the Miyazaki, Fukushima and Iwate Prefectures. A specialised device has been set up in these Prefectures in February 2020, which will monitor communications and analyse them on an ongoing basis using AI.

Technicians will also be sent from Digital Hearts in the event breaches require a visit. Mr Miyazaki, who is a security consultant from Digital Hearts, will try to find out the pricing range for their services that would be acceptable and affordable to the SME companies surveyed.

Japan has been looking to the US and Europe as in the US, for example, the government administration had warned those companies wishing to be part of defence procurement that they must have cybersecurity countermeasures in place. Accordingly, Mr Naota Yokohama of the IPA has warned recently that any Japanese companies without sufficient countermeasures could be removed from supply-chain lists. Mr Yokohama noted that once a breach occurs, which will inevitably have multiple company impact, the company responsible will be found accountable for the breach. He believes the business contract should make it clear but adds the proviso that a number of companies do not even have stipulations concerning cyberattack and risk in their business contracts. In a recent IPA survey on outsourcing, 80% of company respondents answered that their business contracts do not stipulate who is responsible for the new threats of cyberattack.

The latest moves to facilitate security countermeasures to be adopted in supply chain companies include the Ministry of Economy, Trade and Industry facilitating discussions concerning how the sphere of responsibility could be defined. For example, a contract can contain a duty allotment table, which clarifies beforehand the responsibility of maintaining security either by the consignor or consignee. Awareness for cyber countermeasures is now required in business contracts by law.[6]

Prevention of cyberattack

Information sharing

One of the major ways organisations in Japan are mitigating cyber risk and attack whether related to IP theft or cyberwarfare is through information sharing. This method emphasises human communication to be organised to provide a barrier to hackers trying to penetrate cyber systems.

The Cyber Security Council (CSC) in April 2019 explained why such an information sharing approach can be an effective countermeasure. They note that without rapid information sharing of the nature of the cyberattack including the method and countermeasures, the damage and the extent of the attack will proliferate across organisations.

One of the greatest barriers to information sharing was a lack of trust between organisations and concerns that their reputations could be damaged through leaks of information confidential to companies. A significant amendment to the Cybersecurity Act in December 2018 gave rise to the CSC and allowed for legislation to occur that would make it a legal requirement to share information. It was acknowledged by the CSC that companies were affected badly by leaks in information sharing due to the poor handling of such information. Such leaks often led to the breaking of other laws, which further damaged companies. An example of this would be the leaking of sensitive data that could assist a company competitor gaining access to the results of research or IP that had not as yet been patented.

The CSC decided to create compliance legislation that included an obligation of confidentiality when sharing information between companies. Non-compliance enshrined in law meant that leaks would be punished by the perpetrator to be imprisoned for up to one year or fines up to Yen 500,000. The obligation of information sharing was also subject to precise laws and regulation. In addition, a specialised organisation/agency, which was defined by the government ordinance, was entrusted with the running of the information sharing activities for the CSC. It was seen as imperative that an organisation/agency exists to coordinate the information sharing, acting as a contact point to give company members peace of mind.

Cybersecurity Act revision

A document from the National Information Security Center (NISC) provides a summary of the Cybersecurity Act revision and the structure of the CSC.

The legislative Bill to amend parts of Cybersecurity Act includes the following:

- The CSC has been instituted to enable various public and private entities to mutually cooperate in the sharing of cybersecurity information, discussing and implementing of necessary countermeasures in order to ensure cybersecurity takes place and that Japan will be fully prepared for the Tokyo 2021 Olympic Games.
- The first task will be the establishment of a CSC by the Cyber Security Strategy Headquarters, which will allow public and private entities to mutually cooperate in the sharing of information and discussion of required countermeasures. The structure of this organisation will

have its Headquarters at the NISC and have offices at other specialised institutions such as national and local administrative organs, principal infrastructure and cyber entities, educational or research institutions, and among experts.

- Confidentiality, cooperation and information sharing to the council will be ensured as mentioned above, which will facilitate communications with the Headquarters. The administrative functions of this process will be under the jurisdiction of the Headquarters as well. This will include communications with those in Japan and abroad in relating cybersecurity incidents. Parts of these administrative operations will coordinate with entities stipulated in government ordinances, which will also define in detail terms of their obligations to confidentiality not exceeding one year from enactment within the Bill. The CSC is structured in the following manner:

Cyber Security Council
Headquarters (NISC and specialised institutions) **Experts**
Information on threat provided by specialised institutions will be shared strategically and swiftly
National administrative organs | Local authorities | Principal infrastructure entities | Cyber entities (security/system operators) | Educational institutions
All the above entities implementing countermeasures individually
↓
Facilitating to ensure cybersecurity
↓
Ensuring safety and security of the citizens

- Contributing to enhance the smooth functioning of social economic systems in Japan.
- The Council also cooperates with administrative organs and private sectors abroad. [7]

Challenges of information sharing

In June 2019, over 8,000 attendants gathered at Cyber Week 2018, the international conference on cybersecurity, held at Tel Aviv University in Israel. Many of the speakers raised the issue of information sharing as a future challenge. Mr Dorit Dor, Vice President at Check Point,[8] said about the current situtation: 'Information sharing would be insignificant and meaningless unless we share attack methods and context. However, this is a very complex matter and many share only the outcome once attacks have taken place.'

In preparation for cyber physical attacks, the Ben Gurion International Airport developed a state-of-the-art security operation centre three years ago, which incorporates the capacity of real-time detection by utilising AI and also integrates the management systems of both the IT and OT (operations technology) departments. However, information sharing has been kept among those agencies or institutions affiliated to the Airport and it was very rare to share information with those outside the Airport entity. Mr Dor noted that cooperation among attack prevention experts is not sufficient whilst attackers are thought to be using dark webs to strengthen their activity network.

Outsourcing analysis

There is one company that is attempting to achieve cooperation among those who are in charge of attack prevention, by utilising blockchain. PolySwarm, a US start-up, is aiming to create an outsourcing market place for malware analysis where security analysts from the around the globe can participate freely with smart contracts and also get paid incentives in cryptocurrencies. The company gives a picture of future business in which specialists are working together to build an analysis engine and those related are sharing information. It also aims to improve the status of security specialists in order to prevent them from being forced to become attackers for financial reasons.

This type of cooperation between Japanese specialists and those abroad would potentially bring a positive outcome such as enhanced attack prevention and resolution due to lack of cyber risk specialists.

In terms of the use of blockchain in cybersecurity, attention must be paid to security countermeasures in IoT and digital data since blockchain offers high integrity and availaiblity. For example, a blockchain-based e-signature technology, developed by Guardtime in Estonia, is used to detect manipulation and tampering for online services provided by the government and it has proven the usefulness of blockchain. Although blockchain would not solve all issues, there is anticipation it can address some cybersecurity issues.

Societal interdisciplinary involvement

The NCSC in the UK has the Sociotechnical Security Group, where R&D has been carried out by focusing on 'how society becomes involved in technology', not on 'solving issues with technology'. Experts from various fields such as socio-economy, psychology, computing and philosophy engage in discussions to develop the guidance and security tools. In the current circumstance where it is commonly said that cybersecurity is not just a technological issue, this type of approach exploring the involvement of society can provide an inkling to understanding how to engage with the latest technology.[9]

Real-time information sharing

The NISC will be in charge of the administrative office of the CSC and it is planned that parts of administrative tasks will be commissioned to JPCERT/CC (Japan Computer Emergency Response Team /Coordination Center).

To achieve real-time information sharing, the Council will be coordinated through the system, not a physical meeting. (This is applicable to the general meeting and operational committee.)

JPCERT/CC (a system to provide early-warning information) is currently developing CISTA (Collective Intelligent Agents for Trusted Advocates), by collecting a wide range of information, and then sending out notification for early-stage warnings. The Council's system will be based on CISTA, but adds necessary features such as a portal website where information sharing is taking place in real time among members.

To alleviate burdens on its members, the CSC will strengthen cooperation with existing various information sharing systems. The acceptance of information at the Council will be dealt as part of any type of framework in which a member has already participated. However, in the event that members request direct submission of information to the Council, where strict confidentiality is applied, such matters will be handled directly in the future.

Structure of the CSC

The CSC cybersecurity information structure and aims can be seen in Tables 3.1, 3.2 and 3.3.

Table 3.1 Structure for information sharing

Concerns and uncertainty of vendors		*Measures taken with operational rules (T&Cs)*
A wish to disclose the content of information and consultation on a voluntary basis only to those trusted	→	Those who provide information can set up a limit on the extent of information sharing. Such limits will not be changed without consent
A consultation on a voluntary basis may result in punishment by related authorities	→	Those who provide information could exclude related authorities from the extent of information sharing recipients
More information may be requested than expected due to potential application of obligation for information provision	→	A triggering factor of such obligation will be defined and limited expressly in 'a large scale cyberattack' and others
Amendment of the terms and conditions may bring a situation in which all information is requested	→	Amendment of the terms and conditions will require a majority in voting at the general meeting, which consists of all members including private sectors
Termination of the membership of the council may be difficult	→	Members can terminate their membership at any time by submitting a letter

Table 3.2 Council role in information sharing

Issues for specialised institutions and vendors		*Direction the Council takes to resolve issues*
It is difficult to disclose information such as analysis content that has not been proven yet to the outside of the company	→	By making the most of the benefit of the Council such as the obligation to keep confidentiality, which is subject to fines or charges if breached, the Task Force (TF) will be set up in the Council. This special TF will accommodate only a few volunteer members who have a high level of relationship of trust among themselves and can share information mutually, including unproven analysis content
It is not fair for them to keep outputting information because it is valuable	→	The TF will prevent 'free riding' and information sharing will be based on 'give and take'
Valuable information is provided, so appropriate feedback needs to be given	→	The TF will ensure there is a system to provide feedback to information provided without fail

Table 3.3 Organisation of information sharing

The Category 1 group members (corporate entities defined by the government ordinance such as security specialists and vendors)		*The Category 2 group members, ordinal members (national, local administrative organs, principal infrastructure, educational institutions, private sectors) – whether to participate in the Council is left to each entity's will*
① The primary group members will share internally and also exchange feedback regarding the content of analysis that has not been proven as yet in-house with a strong obligation of confidentiality so that the level of accuracy on analysis would be enhanced rapidly and other members would be able to receive information on countermeasures.	→ ① Provision of information including countermeasures (high degree of accuracy) → → ② Provision of information including countermeasures (low degree of accuracy) → ← ② Feedback ← ← ③ Internal consulting ← → ③ Internal advice →	① The members of Category 2 and ordinal members will receive information with a high degree of accuracy that is provided by the Council, and will utilise it for their own organisations' countermeasures. ② In addition, the members of the Category 2 group will be able to receive information including countermeasures, which is given at an earlier stage. (Accuracy is not guaranteed at this

(*continued*)

Table 3.3 Cont.

The Category 1 group members (corporate entities defined by the government ordinance such as security specialists and vendors)	*The Category 2 group members, ordinal members (national, local administrative organs, principal infrastructure, educational institutions, private sectors) – whether to participate in the Council is left to each entity's will*
E.g. Highly specialised analysis • Identifier of vulnerability used in attacks • Malware behaviour E.g. Countermeasures • Special fixes/patches from certain manufacturers • Not using PCs ② The Category 1 members provide information internally on countermeasures that has not been proven as yet with strong obligation of confidentiality to the Category 2 members only. Following their feedback, these Category 1 members will enhance the accuracy level of analysis rapidly. ③ The Category 1 members will also be able to understand what is taking place in the society by dealing with consulting with companies that are affected. ※ Any entity, other than a specialised institution or vendor, that meets criteria and upon request could become the members in the Category 1 group. ※ In the case where any Category 1 member fails to fulfil their contribution requested, such a member will not maintain its status in the group.	stage and obligation of confidentiality is applied.) They will send feedback. ③ The ordinal members and those in the Category 2 group can consult internally with the members of Category 1 group with strong obligation of confidentiality for advice (voluntary). ※ They can request a consultation casually even for a matter they feel unusual intuitively. ※ Any entity regardless of national or local administrative organ, principal infrastructure, educational institution and private sector could become a member of Group 2 once it meets the criteria and upon request. ※ In the case where any Category 2 member fails to fulfil their contribution requested, such a member will not maintain its status in the group.

Sources: All tables compiled from the following: www.jpcert.or.jp/english/, www.nisc.go.jp/active/infra/outline.html, www.ipa.go.jp/files/000032417.pdf, www.jc3.or.jp/media/pdf/pressreleaseEnglish.pdf, www.enisa.europa.eu, www.fsisac.com and www.eisac.com

How activities of the CSC would work

Cybersecurity 2018 and 2019

The Japanese government action plan to deal with cybersecurity consists of two parts (one is an annual report for 2018 as part 1 and a new action plan for 2019 as part 2), and mainly deals with the situation of cybersecurity in Japan in 2018 and the status of policy implementation. The first part contains three major topics such as formulation of a new strategy (27 July 2018), amendments of a group of criteria for information security in governmental organs (25 July 2018) and approaches to information sharing and cooperation that go beyond the existing framework (5 December 2018). The second part focuses on approaches according to policies as well as concrete measures in accordance with the new strategy. An understanding of these strategies is vital to knowing how Japan perceives cyber threat attack and how to implement preventive measures that deal with the risk of IP theft and aspects of cyberwarfare.

Measures for merging cyberspace and physical space

In July 2018, the government formulated a new strategy that aimed to achieve a 'cybersecurity eco system', in which not only the government, critical infrastructure vendors and private sectors but also individual citizens and organisations that use their services are expected to engage in autonomous approaches to cybersecurity. Since 2000, the government and critical infrastructure vendors have been working on various initiatives to enhance and maintain the vitality of economic society. Companies with significant influence on society are considered as key players in implementing cybersecurity measures.

Changing cyberspace and increased seriousness of threats

The new cybersecurity strategy demonstrates the nation's aim and policies of various measures over the next three years including the Tokyo Olympics, which have been provisionally postponed to 2021. Continuous development of cyberspace can only be achieved through improved cybersecurity that operates at all levels of society. This includes digital transformation with cybersecurity, threats and their impact in cyberspace such as through operation and service disruption, information leaks, phishing and fraud as well as ransomware. International events such as the G20 and the Tokyo Olympic Games are vulnerable to cyberattack as they are extraordinary events that draw media attention and have maximum impact in the case of a cyberwarfare attack, for example. AI is also taken into account and there are four categories in AI-related topics such as attacks using AI, autonomous attacks by AI, attacks on AI and security measures using AI. As AI is a relatively new technology possible cyber breaches are explored in relation to issues of liability especially in the event of accidents occurring because of seemingly independent actions taken by AI mechanisms. This could be, for example, an algorithmic quirk in a cyberwarfare robot taking potentially lethal action.

All countermeasures and policies include support for general society within the 'cybersecurity eco system'. This is akin to innovative eco systems in general but in this case one in which the protection afforded by cybersecurity will aid the creation of innovation, which will produce value. This eco system in turn will be used for investment, R&D and human resources, leading to further innovation in society. Each citizen is expected to have awareness and understanding of cybersecurity measures and deal with risks autonomously in their daily life, such as washing their hands to prevent infection or observing traffic lights to prevent a car crash.

Therefore, cyber defence is not only proactive but also integrated fully into society at every level. Implementation of active preventive measures against cyber threats includes the amendment of NICT law (National Institute of Information and Communications Technology). This is an innovative approach in that the law allows for investigation into potentially vulnerable IoT devices before an incident takes place, not after it occurs. Another innovation is the CSC, which accommodates private-sector involvement in addition to governmental bodies and critical infrastructure vendors.[10]

Performance and assessment of cybersecurity measures, 2018

Some of the results of actions taken in 2018 include a workshop of 'cybersecurity management guidelines' and a handbook on information protection, which aims to enhance awareness among corporate executives and senior management. Other actions taken involve a public hearing on 'Cyber physical security measures framework' that is related to safe supply chains, an effort to establish safe IoT systems, provision of an attack early-detection tool through IPA and JPCERT/CC, further strengthening of the information sharing system and risk assessment, protection of IT assets and the research environment in higher education and further promotion of risk management among critical service vendors in preparation for the Olympics. There is also a 'Proven in Japan' concept for verification and assessment of new security technologies including IoT devices in addition to further follow-up work in relation to the already-held Japan–ASEAN (Association of Southeast Asian Nations) cybersecurity policy conference. As for the CSC, its operation commenced from May 2019 with the second and third member application opened in 2019 as well.

The main ministries aimed to achieve in 2019 the enhancement of awareness of cybersecurity, promotion of investment in cybersecurity, strengthening cybersecurity businesses that support innovative promotion of supply chains that produce value, support for SMEs, systematisation and internationalisation of standards in IoT, further protection of critical infrastructure, further promotion of information sharing, international cooperation and collaboration on cybersecurity, promotion of R&D and human resource implementation of cybersecurity awareness throughout all departments.

Risk management practice

In Japan there is concern that the only way to mitigate cyber risk in all its forms and in relation to IP and cyberwarfare is to prepare all those involved so they are an integral part of the countermeasures. Stakeholders as they are referred to in Japan need to exchange both information and opinions on how to work internally to prevent cyberattacks. Both the private sector and the government must work together to protect critical infrastructure.

Promotion of risk communication and consultation is encouraged among top management, cybersecurity departments, departments of control and information systems using IT e.g. operational control (OT) or IoT, user departments and other internal stakeholders.

The CEPTOAR council, which is made up of independent bodies including government organisations, is used for cross-sectoral promotion of the enhancement of information and opinion exchanges in cooperation with diverse stakeholders while collecting information necessary for studies and analyses of new risk sources and risks.

Top-level management are viewed as responsible for showing leadership in cybersecurity matters as individuals contributing to society as a whole. This also means involving all those in their supply chains including business partners, subsidiaries and affiliated companies.

They should also be involved in incident readiness at all times and if an incident occurs, dealing with it promptly from the perspective of gaining trust and encouraging feelings of security among stakeholders. Senior management need to continually procure and maintain budgets, systems and personnel to secure all the above measures and allocate them in the most risk-free manner.

Development of human resources

Experts, as mentioned above, are tasked with raising awareness and promote understanding to top management of critical infrastructure operators presenting cybersecurity measures based on each company's business policies fostering personnel who can bridge critical infrastructure protection related departments within the company to make comprehensive adjustments while leading working-level officials.

Human resource managers are responsible for upgrading cybersecurity measures due to changing circumstances for OT management departments and legal affairs among other relevant departments. IT management departments are only one of many as the emphasis needs to be with organising a structure that straddles all departments and sectors when it concerns cybersecurity countermeasures.

In industry, academia and government collaborations clarifying the definitions of required security experts are necessary while promoting concrete human development measures such as exercises, training and obtaining of qualifications.

There has also been created for all stakeholders involved different levels from 1–5 of perceived severity of cyberattack threat to critical infrastructure. This ranges from:

- Level 5 Emergency for a wide-scale imminent threat.
- Level 4 Severe with a significant impact.
- Level 3 High with a demonstrable effect.
- Level 2 Medium, which may be critical.
- Level 1 Low and unlikely to affect critical infrastructure.[11]

Future of ICT and Japanese cybersecurity

In recent years, the number of cyberattacks, including suspected attempts, is on the rise and the amount of new malware is increasing every year.

The occurrence of new threats lies with new technologies in particular such as AI, IoT and 5G telecommunications systems. As mentioned above, supply-chain companies, usually SMEs, are a particular focus of cyberattacks with IP theft, as shown at the beginning of this chapter, the most frequent target. This is occurring within the context of large-scale cyberattacks in which hackers take advantages through more sophisticated and large-scale attacks utilising new technologies. There is an increase in suspect packets that are being delivered to the NICT monitoring system named Nicter, which shows they are infected with malware, and there is an increase in servers that have been subject to DoS cyberattacks.

A prediction by Symantec is that cyberattackers will be utilising assistance from AI to infiltrate AI systems. This will be especially the case in relation to defence systems and cyberwarfare that will be required to rely more on AI to identify vulnerability and execute countermeasures.

The spheres of attack will become expanded due to the introduction of 5G new-generation telecommunications bandwidth and have been complicated by Chinese telecommunications company Huawei, which the US is banning and Europe is allowing to develop 5G but with caution due to fears of access by the Chinese government to IP, defence data and many other sensitive data bases. This was discussed in Chapter 1 of this book and will be expanded upon in Chapter 5 on China.

It is also predicted by Symantec as by many others conversant with IoT that a new and more dangerous attack than DoS will emerge due to expansion of IoT infrastructure especially between large corporates and their suppliers. This is already leading to a qualitative and quantitative increase in cyberattacks targeting supply chains as mentioned above.

McAfee, in turn, predicted that further utilisation of AI in future preventive technologies would occur with the next target being IoT devices that use voice-recognition features.

Trend Micro also predicts future highly sophisticated targeted attacks that use AI and increased competition among hackers over IoT attacks.

Trends and outlook of the global cybersecurity market and in Japan

With an ever-growing cyber threat, there has been an increased need for cybersecurity products and services. In 2018, the value of the cybersecurity market reached US$ 153 billion and it is estimated to reach US$ 230 billion by 2022. Yet, the market share of Japanese products is relatively small, lagging behind the US and Europe. Foreign companies are also entering into the Japanese market challenging the market share of Japanese cyber goods and services within the Japanese market.

This trend may be seen below in the current status of the Japanese ICT product market share within the global context:

- Base stations: 29% Ericsson (Sweden), 26% Huawei (China), 23.4% Nokia (Finland), 11.7% ZTE (China), 5% Samsung (South Korea)
- Routers (product share in 3Q 2018): US 60%, Europe 27%, China 6.8%, Japan 4.6% and others 1.2%
- Server products (product share in 4Q 2018): US 68.7%, China 26.3% and Japan 5%
- Smartphones: Chinese products 57.4%, US 20.8%, South Korea 18.8%, Japan 1.2% and others 1.8%

Comparison of R&D between foreign companies and Japanese companies

- Companies listed in top ranking include global companies such as Amazon and Alphabet, both of which spend more than 10% of profits on R&D. Chinese companies also follows this trend.
- Japanese companies spend less than 10%, except for the healthcare sector.

Global ranking of R&D spending

Global R&D spending shows the leaders as Amazon, Alphabet, VW, Samsung, Intel, Microsoft, Apple, Roche, Johnson and Johnson and Merck as the top ten companies, with the Japanese company Toyota as eleventh in the global rankings.

Japanese ranking of R&D spending

The top ten companies in Japan in terms of amount spent on R&D are Toyota, Honda, Nissan, Sony, Panasonic, Denso, Hitachi, Takeda, Canon and Toshiba in ranked order. The first three are automotive manufacturing companies.

Chinese ranking of R&D spending

Chinese companies in ranked order are Alibaba, Tencent and Baidu, which have been spending about 10% of all profits on R&D since 2013. There are only three but all relate to the internet.

Environment surrounding start-ups and Japan's presence

New companies that develop advanced technologies to tackle cyberattacks have been set up but most are based in the US and Israel.

Japanese companies have failed to be ranked in the cybersecurity sector leaving them vulnerable to both cyberattack and economically. Abenomics, which began in 2013 with a three-pronged strategy that included monetary and fiscal stimulus in addition to structural reforms, has failed to produce results needed for innovation and growth in the Japanese economy. A new package of fiscal stimuli amounting in real terms to £182 billion (Yen 13.2 trillion) was introduced by Prime Minister Abe in December 2019 to counter a low expansion rate of 0.2% in the third quarter of 2019 and a collapse in retail sales as consumers reacted adversely to a new consumption tax. The history of consumption taxes in Japan is that they depress severely consumer confidence with retail sales falling significantly. There is also concern that without substantive investment in innovation, temporary growth from the Tokyo Olympics in 2021 will fall again after the event is finished.[12]

However, there are some start-ups specialising in cybersecurity in Japan through a venture/start-up support system that was initiated during Prime Minister Koizumi's administration initiatives.[13] If Koizumi's son runs for Prime Minister and wins the next election there is a good chance that start-up initiatives will be re-started. In the last 20 years one of Japan's most innovative projects, a biotech start-up in Tsuruoka, Yamagata Prefecture is now an innovation high-tech cluster, which has also prevented the town of Tsuruoka from disappearing because of little or no employment prospects for younger people who moved to Tokyo. It all began when Professor Masuru Tomita from Keio University was asked to start a science laboratory in the feudal, agricultural town of Tsuruoka. Opposition from the local population was fierce as their taxpayer money was to be spent supporting this research initiative. The Mayor Yoichi Tomizuka was very visionary and courageous as he insisted this project should proceed. It now is home to several world-class innovative enterprises including Spiber Ltd, which has through R&D created synthetic spider silk. A report published in March 2019 stated that the Science Park has generated Yen 3 billion per annum and created over 500 new jobs.

All Professor Tomita's colleagues had predicted that the new Science Park project would collapse because it was not based in Tokyo but, to the contrary, he notes it has flourished because of the tranquility, fresh air and good food. Also as an incentive for the local community, a new hotel complex and indoor children's playground was built. As the old Japanese proverb states,'the ship turns around slowly!'[14]

Evidence that Japan is lagging behind is that there are only three Japanese companies among the top 500 cybersecurity companies. Even among the most growth-friendly cities globally for ICT/cybersecurity start-ups, Japanese cities are not included in the list (top 12) of New York, Boston, Silicon Valley, Phoenix, Toronto-Waterloo, Ottawa, Hague, Frankfurt, Berlin, Prague, Tel Aviv and Be'er Sheva.

A start-up initiative in Japan is J-Startup, a programme designed to support start-ups, aiming to make them become competitive globally with innovative technologies and business models that create new value. Members, for example, include Preferred Network (development and offering of deep-learning framework) and Caulis (business to business unauthorised access detection service).

Potential security threat from 5G

Given the demand for change in capacity through the introduction of 5G, the introduction and expansion of network capacity means that increased traffic lends itself to a greater number of cyberattacks. Multiple connections will also give rise to large-scale bots and low latency will prioritise lower overheads, which will lead to lowered security. Finally, converting infrastructure into software and the use of third-party apps will also increase vulnerability.

It is predicted that the potential threats will involve DoS and large-scale DoS cyberattacks bringing unauthorised access and interception.

Trends in standardisation and countermeasures

With the advent of 5G, reliability will be secured in new technologies such as SLICE to establish security assessment criteria. While increased threats due to mega capacity and multiple connections will be dealt with through early detection and energy/automation through AI, there will also be the introduction and application of virtual network functions service/security assessment to prevent vulnerability in addition to an early detection of security events in 5G to prevent a threat from becoming evident.

There will be an automated resolution of a detected event to prevent damage from remaining for a long period of time.

Cybersecurity R&D in USA, UK, Israel and Singapore

In a comparison, the USA, UK, Israel and Singapore were found to have more advanced cybersecurity R&D than Japan.

In the USA the '2016 Federal Cybersecurity Research and Development Strategic Plan' defines the four categories of Deter, Protect, Detect and Adapt and gives short-, medium- and long-term R&D approaches to each category. Every year, an implementation roadmap is formulated. Industry, the government and academia collaborate to promote R&D in the National Institute of Standards and Technology (NIST), the National Science Foundation (NSF), the NSA, the Defense Advanced Research Projects Agency (DARPA), the DHS and the Department of Defense (DoD). The 2019 budget was US$ 740 million.

In the UK the 'National Cyber Security Strategy 2016–2021' has (1) Defend, (2) Deter and (3) Development, the last of which references R&D. It has identified the important areas of IoT, the smart city, data and information protection, automation, machine learning and AI in its 'cyber security science and technology strategy'. Under the framework of Academic Centre of Excellence (ACE) and the initiative of the government, universities that have passed the approval criteria are leading the promotion of R&D.

The 'Israel Cyber Security Strategy' has (1) Robustness, (2) Resilience and (3) Defence. R&D is positioned as part of capacity development to enable these aims. The Israeli government has established a cybersecurity research centre that focuses on various areas of policy and technology at Ben-Gurion University and Tel Aviv University.

There are four pillars in Singapore that support cybersecurity R&D: (1) flexible infrastructure development, (2) maintenance of safer cyberspace, (3) development of an active cyber eco system and (4) strengthening international partnership. R&D is positioned in point 3. The Singaporean government formulated an implementation plan until 2020 in its 'National Cybersecurity R&D Programme'. The Singapore cybersecurity consortium operates as a collaborative organisation between industry, the government and academia

Federal cybersecurity R&D strategic plan in the USA

The '2016 Federal Cybersecurity Research and Development Strategic Plan' identifies the most relevant areas of R&D to focus on. It formulates an implementation plan on an annual basis and promotes it to industry, the government and academic institutions.

The plan defines four categories of R&D focus which are Deter, Protect, Detect and Adapt while providing short-term, medium-term and long-term R&D approaches. In addition, the following areas will be focused on as advanced technology to make the above categories more comprehensive:

1. Cyber physical systems especially IoT
2. Cloud computing
3. High-capacity calculation
4. Autonomous systems
5. Mobile devices

The four categories are as follows.

Short term

Deter

- Measurement criteria of attack levels
- Assessment of relationships between prevention of attack and criminal/economic sanctions

Protect

- Development of secure update mechanisms
- Evidence assessment technologies
- Lightweight encryption, private databases, quantum-proof cryptography

Detect

- Automation tool for mapping networks
- User interface improvement in security operation tools

Adapt

- Technologies that allow for continuous use of important assets in the case of an attack

Medium term

Deter

- Real-time attribution

Protect

- Static/dynamic analytical tool to reduce vulnerability
- A tool that automates the extraction of security policy
- A tool and technology that verifies the authenticity of software and hardware at 98%

Detect

- Identifying malicious cyber activities (reduction of false positive rate, false negative rate)

Adapt

- A timely recovery of features of mutually dependent systems

Long term

Deter

- Accurate and efficient identification of an attacker

Protect

- A tool that supports development of software with one fault per 100,000-line code
- Enhancing effectiveness and efficiency of security control with two-digit orders in ten years

Detect

- Automated cyber threat prediction tool

Adapt

- Adaptive and effective collective defence

ACE in the UK

In the UK the promotion of cybersecurity R&D is within the framework of the ACE, which consists of universities that have passed the approval criteria of the NCSC and Engineering and Physical Sciences Research Council (EPSRC).

In 2001, the EPSRC and GCHQ (Government Communications Headquarters) commenced the ACE framework for the purpose of enhancing resilience against cyberattacks. The NCSC has since taken this remit from GCHQ.

The number of participating universities is 17 as of January 2019. Funding of approximately £20,000 is awarded annually to approved universities such as Queens University in Belfast, Bristol University, Royal Holloway, Newcastle University and Imperial College London.

The key areas of R&D at these UK universities are the following:

- Encryption, key management and related protocol
- Information risk management
- System engineering and security analysis
- Methodology of information warranty

- Operation warranty technology
- Research of strategic technologies and product safety
- Cybersecurity and science of human factors
- Reliability and establishment of a highly reliable system

The approaches of ACE-approved universities are the following:

Imperial College London: Secure and resilient software system engineering including operation systems and information assurance/security analysis and system verification

Newcastle University: Cybercrime using social technology, security assurance of infrastructure, cybersecurity science

Queen's University Belfast: Cyber physical system security, real-time network analysis and virtualisation, high-spec/low-energy consumption cryptography architecture

Royal Holloway: Logical and practical encryption applications, social, technological and organisational perspectives of cybersecurity, information assurance of RFID (Radio-Frequency Identification) tag, smart tag and implanted devices

Israel's cybersecurity eco system

Israel has a unique cybersecurity eco system through the military, the government, industry and academic institutions and accommodates the Cyber Spark, which produces many start-ups, and the academic, which concentrates on cybersecurity research.

Academic eco system with its origin in the security area

A cybersecurity research centre has been initiated at six universities including Ben-Gurion University and Tel Aviv University, which focuses on various areas such as policy and technology and the academic eco system. The driver of the eco system is investment in cybersecurity in the national defence area.

In relation to producing future employees who are cyber aware to a high standard, education is the key. This begins at the middle-school level and continues with expert training during military service human resources. Once students who show aptitude for cyber studies graduate from high school and begin serving in the military, they are sent to cyber-related departments to gain further expert knowledge. After leaving the military, they will work at universities and in the private sector.

Establishment of the Cyber Spark

Under the initiative of Prime Minister Netanyahu and the National Cyber Agency, the Cyber Spark was established at Be'er Sheva in 2014, which forms a cluster, aiming to be an active eco system. Companies and ventures such as Deutsche Telekom, EMC, Lockheed Martin, Oracle, IBM and JVP have their offices at the Cyber Spark and there are many start-ups.

Singapore's national cybersecurity R&D

The National University of Singapore and National Research Foundation are leading cybersecurity R&D institutions based on the 'Cybersecurity R&D Programme' started in 2013. In 2016, the Singapore cybersecurity consortium was established as an organisation for collaboration between industry, the government and academia for the purpose of R&D, human resources and awareness of cybersecurity.

The six themes in R&D areas that are focused on are outlined below. A budget of US$ 190 million is allocated until 2020.

1. Scalable trustworthy systems
2. Resilient systems
3. Effective situation awareness and attack attribution
4. Combatting insider threats
5. Threats detection, analysis and defence
6. Efficient and effective digital forensics

Innovation as key to success

Japan, although suffering from theft of its IP through cyberattack, has also the corresponding problem of not investing enough or creating new innovations to sustain a strong economy. When it does allow innovative ideas to come to the fore such as the Tsuruoka Science Park innovation that not only creates brilliant new inventions but also revitalises regions that are losing their youth to Tokyo, there is great resistance to such innovative ideas. Cyberwarfare is not an immediate threat as Japan tries to keep itself geo-politically neutral and the culture is a closed one that would not easily be affected by election interference and disinformation campaigns by foreign powers.

Notes

1. See Ruth Taplin, *Decision-Making and Japan: A Study of Corporate Japanese Decision-making and Its Relevance to Western Companies*, Abingdon: Routledge, 1995 and 2016. First published by Oriental Library in 1995.
2. 'Japan's cybersecurity tsar admits he has never touched a computer', *The Japan Times*, Richard Lloyd Parry (15 November 2018).
3. See Ruth Taplin, *Decision-Making and Japan: A Study of Corporate Japanese Decision-making and Its Relevance to Western Companies*, Abingdon: Routledge, 2016.

4 See Ruth Taplin, *Decision-Making and Japan: A Study of Corporate Japanese Decision-making and Its Relevance to Western Companies*, Abingdon: Routledge, 2003, second printing, p. 28.
5 'Digital trend – cybersecurity measures in SMEs, thorough preparation at 4%. A blind spot in supply chain', Mari Ishibashi, *Nihon Kezai Shimbun* (2 July 2019). See https://en.digitalhearts.com/
6 Ibid.
7 This information concerning the CSC was found on www.cas.go.jp/jp/houan/180308/siryou1.pdf
8 See www.checkpoint.com/about-us/leadership/
9 This information may be found in 'ICT – World Trends Part 12, Latest technologies in security – Part 2' by Research Fellow Kenji Kobayashi (NEC) at IISE. I met with Professor Kobayashi and his colleagues during my research visit to Japan funded by the Great Britain Sasakawa Foundation in April 2019. He sent to me this account of his global travels to understand the information sharing challenges for Japan. My thanks to him for this information.
10 See www.nisc.go.jp/eng/pdf/cs-senryaku2018-zentaigaiyou-en.pdf
11 *The Cybersecurity Policy for Critical Infrastructure Protection,* Cybersecurity Security Headquarters, Government of Japan (25 July 2018); *Cybersecurity Strategy*, Article 12, Paragraph 4 of the Basic Act on Cybersecurity (27 July 2018). See also www.nisc.go.jp/eng/pdf/cs-senryaku2018-zentaigaiyou-en.pdf
12 'Abe throws billions more at staving off Japan slowdown', Philip Aldrick, *The Times* (6 December 2019).
13 See Ruth Taplin, *Intellectual Property and the New Japanese Global Economy*, London: Routledge, 2009.
14 'Defying local skepticism and "Tokyo first" mentality, Science Park thrives in rural Yamagata', Tomohiro Osaki, *The Japan Times* (6 December 2019).

4 Russia

Cyberwarfare and disinformation

Russia's main use of cyberattack is to re-assert itself as a major global geopolitical force that keeps its own population subdued and reduces the threat of any interference to its leaders' hegemony politically. IP theft does not seem to be a priority as political hegemony is the goal rather than relying on innovation for the economy to expand. Russia holds unrivalled natural resources such as gas reserves and mineral resources, which are controlled by state-run oligarchs who are linked to the ruling inner circle.

Internal control a priority

Russia's operates a relatively low-cost technology to control the domestic internet, which can be replicated easily elsewhere in the world and used in cyberwarfare that allows Russian rulers to politically interfere around the world. Russian surveillance technology relies on a repressive legal network, intimidation of governmental and private companies, ad-hoc monitoring and much less on mass filtering. This means that it is low cost and effective as it works through existing institutional structures and organisations rather than having to create new ones at great expense.

This means that Russians, on the face of it, have access to Facebook, Google and other social media. To control domestic access in real terms the Russian leadership built their digital surveillance infrastructure on open digital spaces. To do this effectively the Soviet-era System of Operative Search Measures (SORM), which was used to spy on telephone calls, was re-instituted in 1995 to monitor all e-mails and online browsing. Most companies to date are now legally required to install SORM equipment. Such companies include internet service providers, social media platforms and telecommunications firms.

SORM does not block information but rather gives backdoor access to Kremlin-controlled security services and government agencies to all data that flows through the internet. Such data access can include internet protocol addresses, the real names of social media users and e-mail addresses of all political opposition when they are planning to organise opposition rallies.

SORM equipment has been sold by Russian companies all over the world, especially those that wish to surveil their domestic populations such as Belarus, Kazakhstan and the Ukraine as well as other countries in Latin America, the Middle East and Africa. MFI Soft is one of the largest suppliers of SORM equipment offering a number of packages and a 24-hour customer service. One of the most sought-after packages is called SORMovich, which can be bought for roughly US$ 20,000. MFI Soft in 2017 became incorporated into the Citadel group of Russian so-called information security companies, which would allow the Kremlin to expand capabilities and standardise pricing.

In any geo-political conflict SORM equipment controlled by the Kremlin gives it information gathering control not just over its own population but also over countries in which it is installed. In the case of cyberwarfare this would give the Kremlin an ideal platform to plan cyberattacks, data mining to influence political outcomes or to consolidate attack plans.[1]

Runet global internet alternative

In 2019 Russia successfully tested Runet, unplugging the Russian-controlled internet from the global internet. Russian users would not have been aware of what was occurring during the test but results would have been given to President Putin. The Russian public had the situation explained to them through the major newspaper *Pravda* and local newspapers quoting the Deputy Minister of Communications, Alexey Sokolov, who described the tests as dealing with emerging cyber risks and threats ensuring the stability of the internet and a unified telecommunications system in the Russian Federation. TASS, the government news agency, reported that the test showed the Russian internet robust enough to stop cyberattack through the IoT and from external influences that may be negative.

Russia is also developing bespoke services such as a Russian version of Wikipedia and also passed a legislative bill that banned the sale of smartphones that did not first have Russian software installed.

There have been many protests against the Russian unplugged internet from the global internet, especially when in March 2019 the Kremlin passed cyber-security bills that many Russians believe are not targeted at protection from cyberattack externally but will be used to limit information sources to the Russian population. The so-called Digital Sovereignty Bill, which the Russian government claims will reduce reliance on US-based internet servers, was challenged by protesters who believe the Bill will increase censorship by the Kremlin and stifle dissent as well as freedom of speech. Other bills passed in March 2019 included the banning of internet conversation that 'disrespects' the Russian authorities or that promotes 'fake news' as defined by them. Campaigners in 2019 also protested about the media watchdog trying to close the encrypted messaging system Telegram because the FSB stated that it was a favoured service of international terrorists.[2]

Cyberattacks and cyberwarfare

The Chief of the Defence Staff in Britain, Sir General Nick Carter, explained how the digital age has served to blur the distinction between war and peace, making cyberattack warfare a daily occurrence. Russia was singled out in particular for creating a cyberwarfare based on competition for power and ideology.

US General Petraeus noted that Russia was revanchist or trying reprise former glory days when it was an international power player not subservient to the US. General Carter noted that Russia is much more of a threat today than it was five years ago because it realises that physical warfare is receding, being replaced by domination of information and the ability to deploy it to the hacker's advantage through controlling its dissemination. He stated clearly that future warfare will be based on control and adept use of information.

General Carter noted that NATO will have to adapt to the biggest future challenges since the Cold War era and that involves preparing the military to understand and be trained to fight cyberwarfare battles. President Putin has been a great catalyst according to both General Carter and General Petraeus in making NATO aware of the new emerging cyberwarfare battle already here and to come.

A key to cyberwarfare they both agreed is disinformation and denying being the source of such duplicitous information. Such tactics presented difficulties for the US and UK military, which have been guided by the rule of law and judged by a court of public opinion. General Carter viewed bringing back the lost art of deceptive tactics as central to combating Russian cyberattacks that are now an integral part of increased cyberwarfare.[3]

Social media used by Russians

To vindicate the explanations of the two generals of how Russia is leading the cyberwarfare campaign of disinformation to reprise its perceived role of former geo-political dominance, social media has become awash with Russian disinformation.

In January 2019, Facebook had to delete about 500 pages of misleading information campaigns targeting Europe and Central Asia that were directly linked mainly to employees of Sputnik. Sputnik is an agency controlled by the Kremlin that was established to disseminate favourable information about Russia globally. Its use of deception is intensive as it spreads disinformation through seemingly innocuous news items related to travel, sports and even the weather. It leaks disinformation through pretending to provide useful, unbiased news items to often gullible readers.

Nathaniel Gleicher, Head of Cybersecurity at Facebook, stated that they are constantly trying to detect people using manipulative tactics to promote their disinformation schemes through content such as seemingly genuine articles and videos. There is also the problem of fake accounts being created in different countries other than Russia with the sole purpose of sharing content with Sputnik. In 2016 during the US presidential election it became abundantly clear that Facebook served as a major platform to influence voters through disinformation, sow divisions and target particular groups of voters. Facebook believes that it is difficult to detect all the disinformation on a platform of two billion users.

Facebook has been trying to trace and delete fake and misinformation accounts originating from Sputnik. In August 2019, Facebook removed 652 fake accounts originating with Russian groups to counter attempts to influence US elections and other misinformation. However, as with cyberwarfare, this is an ongoing battle with Russian agencies related to the Kremlin becoming ever more deceptive and sophisticated in such deceit.

The Atlantic Council's Digital Forensic Research Lab found that on a single day in October 2017, Sputnik content was created to target Armenia, Chechnya, Estonia, Georgia, Latvia, Lithuania, Kyrgyzstan and Tajikistan. There were also fan pages purporting to support the presidents of Uzbekistan and Tajikistan created, but they were actually run from Russia.[4]

Part of the Russian cyberwarfare strategy is to target the greatest number of people in many countries through social media giants, bombarding them with deceitful cyber misinformation.

Cyberwarfare enters Latin America

Latin American countries are the latest to be the target of Russian-backed cyberwarfare through social media. The cyber influence campaigns began a decade ago in tandem with digital technology and the rise in social media use. Russia has become one of the strongest allies of President Maduro in Venezuela and has been using that country as a springboard for spreading conspiracy theories, disinformation and even outright falsehoods to undermine liberal, democratic policies.

Two Spanish-language, Russian-based news organisations have been at the forefront of such disinformation activities in Latin American countries. One is Sputnik Mundo, a Spanish-language arm of Sputnik mentioned above, which is produced partly in Montevideo, Uruguay and began broadcasting in the last few years. The other is RT (Russian Television) Espanol, which states it reaches 18 million people in ten Latin American countries every week and has over a billion views on YouTube.

Evidence of Russian interference in Latin American countries' political affairs is growing. In Bolivia, for example, Russian-backed tweets were fewer than five a day but around the time President Evo Morales was pressured to resign on 10 November 2019, Russian-based Twitter accounts rose to over 1,000. It was also found over one 30-day period in Bolivia, Ecuador, Columbia, Chile and Peru that Russian-backed accounts sent out very similar messages within 90 minutes of each other.[5]

Rogue cybercriminal hackers/mercenaries

It is not always the Russian government that hacks into international systems. There are highly trained Russians conversant with digital technology who, unable to find work with government agencies, work on their own building networks to defraud companies and individuals globally driven by pecuniary concerns. If IP theft delivers them a worthwhile return on their time, they will steal IP. If working as cyber mercenaries involves easy monetary gain, they will hire themselves out to the highest bidder. This is potentially how Russian hackers/mercenaries could contribute to cyberwarfare in the future.

A criminal cybercrime gang called GozNym was started in 2007 by five Russian hackers. The name is a hybrid of two pieces of malware: Gozi and Nymaim. The first piece acts as a dropper software that enters or drops into a computer system, installing malware. Until 2015 it was mainly used to install ransomware. The other piece of this hybrid used a variety of techniques over the years to mine financial data globally, although largely in the US. The Russian cybercriminals used gang members in the US, Germany, Bulgaria, Moldova, Georgia and the Ukraine to steal from bank accounts, money launder and defraud banks. In all, before they were caught and prosecuted, they stole US$ 100 million (£77 million) from more than 40,000 victims including international corporations, SMEs, law firms and NGOs. In a cross-border cooperation between Europol and law-enforcement agencies in the US, all but the initial five Russian hackers were caught and tried with the international gang dismantled. The five Russian nationals who were not apprehended were found to be making money and spreading the cyber mechanisms of the crime through leasing GozNym to other cybercriminals worldwide.

Russian cybercriminals seem able to slip back into their country and disappear more effectively than in many other countries. Yet, they do not seem to have the protection of the Kremlin and non-Russian members of the gang can be caught as in this example. It is quite possible they will re-emerge in a different guise, maybe as cyberwarfare mercenaries.[6]

Geo-political interference

The Russian government and its agencies are proving much more difficult to catch than their home-grown cybercriminals as they operate through deceit and denial.

In October 2019, the NSA and its British counterpart issued a warning that the Russians have returned and with an increased stealth. Russian government intelligence agencies, they noted, had been hacking into the network of high-level Iranian intelligence agency units attacking governments and private companies in Britain and the Middle East attempting to create havoc by having Teheran blamed.

For those state and federal administrative officials who are tasked with safeguarding the 2020 US elections, it is becoming clear that a Russian-directed election cyberwar will be different than the one carried out in 2016. Russian stealth is increasing and the Russians attaching themselves to Iranian networks is a sign of the deceitful tactics of hacking and disinformation to come in the US 2020 elections. The Russian government can easily blame another country for its own interference, much like attempting to blame Ukraine for Russia's election meddling.

US defences against cyberattack have improved hugely since the 2016 cyberwar waged by Russia. Facebook, a prime carrier of disinformation is now, as mentioned above, much more aware of tactics such as fake ads being paid for in rubles or calls for California, the world's sixth largest economy, to secede from the union, with this movements' headquarters being based in Moscow. Facebook is searching for and deleting such disinformation. Likewise, officials who oversee voting have been familiarising themselves with how cyberattacks are carried out through malware and bots, for example. In addition, military officials, as mentioned above, are considering engaging in information cyberwarfare and even in retaliating by hacking into senior Russian officials' accounts.

Yet, many of the cyber vulnerabilities that US elections faced in 2016 not only remain but also have become stealthier. A major issue that has changed, however, is that in 2020 Russian disinformation and troll cyberattacks are no longer a new surprise that American political parties and voting officials had no idea were imminent.[7]

A number of problems remain that affected the election in 2016. One is that political campaigns are unwilling to spend the amounts needed for effective cyber defences. The second is that social media, the messages emanating from the White House and certain news channels confuse the electorate with misleading stories and cries of fake news plus the increasing inability of many voters to be able to distinguish between fact and reality denial. Much of social media, cult-like figures and peddlers of conspiracy theories blur the lines between fact and fiction.

Therefore, the burden often falls on vigilant, well-trained election officials to detect cyberattacks that can disrupt full and fair access to facts about the candidates that are free from damaging doubts sowed by Russian- or now Iranian-backed stealth misinformation campaigns.

Obstacles to fighting electoral cyberattack

After the cyberattack on Hillary Clinton's presidential campaign by the Russians in 2016, political parties have been attempting to strengthen their cyber defences. The current obstacle to finding the most effective cybersecurity service is the federal law that stipulates private, corporate security companies cannot offer free or discounted cybersecurity services to federal candidates. If political parties wish to offer their candidates cybersecurity services, this law also prohibits such actions as they are deemed in-kind donations.

The Federal Election Commission blocked an offer in 2019 from Area 1, a Silicon Valley cybersecurity firm, to offer discounted cyber defence services to 2020 presential candidates. Senator Ron Wyden introduced a bill soon after that ruling that would have allowed all political parties to offer their candidates expert cybersecurity assistance but the Senate majority leader Mitch McConnell stopped it and any like bills from even being voted on. This was despite the warning from FBI Director Christopher Wray in April 2019 that Russian counterintelligence efforts to disrupt the 2020 US presidential elections remain a real and continued threat.

Cyber risk is a great obstacle for presidential candidates trying to run for federal office who, unlike corporations, do not have hundreds of millions of dollars to hire cybersecurity experts. Laura Rosenberger, the Director of the Alliance for Securing Democracy (a group that both tries to track and expose attempts by authoritarian regimes to undermine democratic elections) states that allowing presidential candidates to fend for themselves without any extra, expert assistance that can employ the latest technology such as cyber defence countermeasures is posing challenging obstacles to free and fair elections. Laura Rosenberger has first-hand experience of such cyberattacks as she was foreign policy advisor to Hillary Clinton during her 2016 presidential campaign when Russian hackers mounted a spear-phishing campaign that compromised Clinton's Campaign Chairman John Podesta's e-mails in addition to those of the Democratic Congressional Campaign Committee.

With Russia, as mentioned above, through state actors and individual criminals showing the way or actually selling the hacking technology, there is great scope for authoritarian rogue states, stateless actors and domestic terrorists to interfere in the 2020 elections, which are so important to world economic and geo-political stability.

Given these inherent risks, the Federal Election Commission in May 2020 ruled that that a non-profit company founded by two bi-partisan former campaign managers called Defending Digital Campaigns can offer its services to presidential candidates.

Area 1 attempted to apply to offer its breakthrough new anti-phishing technology but it was Microsoft that was given permission to offer cyber defence services to its clients as it was for business purposes only. The Federal Election Commission has a very difficult decision to make because a less than cautious approach could open the door to corporations or other businesses wishing to offer cybersecurity services while really wanting to affect the election outcome.[8]

In fact, cybersecurity issues for the Democratic caucuses in Iowa in February 2020 have caused such concern over cyberattack that the DNC sent their best disinformation and cybersecurity specialists. This was to ensure that the caucuses do not experience hacking and serious disinformation, which can influence who will become the Democratic presidential candidates. The DNC is concerned that Russia or even Iran will try to influence the outcome in their favour.

Yet, after the failure of the high-tech app used to count votes as those volunteering to run the election fairly had little understanding of how to make the new app work, when they attempted to contact those organising the app on a bespoke helpline they could not reach anyone as the lines were overwhelmed with other equally bewildered election volunteers trying to reach for help. The backup in the end that was relied on consisted of paper presidential preference sheets. There is a call now to revert to this 19th-century technology in the future for fair, Russian hacking-free results.[9,10]

The role of Cyber Command

To cope and counter very serious cyberwarfare attacks including potential and actual physical infrastructural ones and political ones to do with subsequent elections, the US Cyber Command was given legal sweeping powers to deal with the Russian cyber threat. In August 2018, President Trump signed a much-anticipated executive order named National Security Presidential Memorandum 13. The essence of this Congress-generated executive order was that Cyber Command would be enabled to carry out all types of countermeasures that also included infiltrating foreign networks without presidential approval. This was a practical move as US computer networks were under such intensive attack that the Cyber Command required unfettered access to the foreign networks, such as the Russians' in this case to speedily counter such cyber intrusions into all areas of American life. Congress authorised this freedom of action as Cyber Command was viewed as part of the regular military, which included cyberspace, and their work was to be viewed as carrying out ordinary patrols.

Once given the authority, the Cyber Command attacked the Russian intelligence units responsible for the bulk of the US election hacking. During the time of the subsequent mid-term elections, they also shut down the Internet Research Agency in St Petersburg, which had been responsible for designing disinformation social media ads such as those that were found on Facebook.

Cyber Command also targeted the GRU, the Russian military intelligence responsible for breaking into the DNC making their private data public. They also sent text messages to Russian hackers and officials warning them that they knew who they were and where to find them if they continued to make trouble for US elections and politics in general. Much of this action was made public.

There is a good deal of discussion and concern of the role Russia will play in influencing the 2020 US elections. Will they exploit the COVID-19 pandemic to boost the fortunes of incumbent Trump? Will the Russian intelligence service SVR, the counterpart to the US primary intelligence agency the CIA, become more involved in the US election disinformation campaign than the Russian military intelligence agency, the GRU? As it was the GRU that was caught meddling in the 2016 elections, perhaps the more skilled SVR will take the lead? Such political intelligence movements have direct implications for the extent and success of IP theft as outlined in this chapter and the use of cyberattack as a means for military domination in the increasing move towards cyberwarfare.[11]

Public grid retaliation

What the public has been less aware of was a covert action by the US using cyber tools to place codes inside the Russian power grid where they would not be seen but which were there in the event the US needed to undermine Russian utilities. Russians already had the capability to undermine US utilities by placing malware codes in them. The US now had the same possibility to destroy Russian utilities by placing a ticking time bomb that could be unleashed if the conflict between the two countries deteriorated into cyberwarfare with tangible physical infrastructural effects.

These acts of potentially highly damaging infrastructural destruction could be as deadly as bombing in that huge numbers of civilians in hospitals or care homes without electricity could quickly die. The Russians, as do other countries such as Iran, do not wish to enter full-scale war with the US. It is too dangerous for all involved. Therefore, to date, cyberwarfare is being used by the Russians as short-term warfare to have limited and subtle effects such as interfering in elections while pretending not to and supporting candidates that are favourable to Russia.[12]

Therefore, the situation between Russia and its main adversary, the US, is manifested as a war of attrition, unlikely to break out into major cyberwarfare for the foreseeable future. Yet, examples of Russian interference can be seen all around the world, using cyber tools to gain geo-political influence and power over many countries not as advanced in cyberattack.

This may still be at the stage of the nuclear deterrent option of we need to have one to stop being attacked by another entity, but will not use such a lethal option.

However, cyber tools are being used to develop clothing and robots to perhaps engage in an actual physical cyberwar. At present, it is still a war of attrition and AI, the subject of the follow-on book from this one, may have a determining role in such an outcome. In a subsequent chapter (Chapter 7) we will also deal with the vulnerability of power grids to cyberattack and the importance of keeping safe from such cyber risk and attack.

Notes

1 'Russia is teaching the world to spy: easy-to-use technology straight from Moscow for any aspiring strongman – at a low price', Alina Polyakova, *New York Times* (5 December 2019).

2 'Russia successfully tests its "unplugged internet"', *BBC News* (24 December 2019). 'Russia internet freedom: thousands protest against cyber-security bill', *BBC News* (10 March 2019).

3 'Britain is "at war every day" due to constant cyber attacks, Chief of the Defence Staff says', Dominic Nicholls, *The Telegraph* (29 September 2019).

4 'Facebook identifies Russia-linked misinformation campaign', Adam Satariano, *New York Times* (17 January 2019).
5 'As protests in South America surged, so did Russian trolls on Twitter, U.S. finds', Lara Jakes, *New York Times* (19 January 2020).
6 'GozNym cyber-crime gang which stole millions busted', Jane Wakefield, Technology Reporter, *BBC News* (16 May 2019).
7 '"Chaos is the point": Russian hackers and trolls grow stealthier in 2020', Victor J. Blue, *New York Times* (10 January 2020).
8 'The only safe election is a low-tech election', Kevin Roose, *New York Times* (4 February 2020).
9 'Election rules are an obstacle to cybersecurity of presidential campaigns', Nicole Perlroth and Matthew Rosenberg, *New York Times* (6 June 2019).
10 'DNC heads to Iowa to help protect caucuses from digital attacks and disinformation', Erin Ayers, *Advisen Cyber News, Digest Edition* (31 January 2020).
11 'Can Russia use the coronavirus to sow discord among Americans?', Thomas Rid, *New York Times* (16 March 2020).
12 'US escalates online attacks on Russia's power grid', David E. Sanger and Nicole Perlroth, *New York Times* (15 June 2019).

5 China

China (People's Republic of China or PRC) and its acolyte state North Korea use cyberattack and hacking, mainly on the state level, for a wide variety of purposes. The major use is to steal IP to keep up with advances in technology in the US, UK and other Western-allied countries with advanced technology such as Israel. As a good deal of the IP stolen has to do with military technology, the other use is to become militarily dominant through cyberwarfare tactics on a geo-political level.

IP theft

There is a pattern of behaviour that typifies China's theft of IP. The Department of Justice (DoJ) has been investigating IP theft for more than a decade. The Obama administration reached an agreement with China to halt this theft. In due course China no longer honoured this agreement leading to increased IP theft and the use of trade talks and punitive tariffs to try to force China to agree to stop stealing US IP.

Yet, using trade talks such as those of the trade meeting of the World Trade Organization (WTO) in December 2018, when the United States accused China of circumventing the law to advance its economic interests, did not accord with the views of law-enforcement officers.

While perhaps agreeing in principle that China engages unfair advantage through subsidising and maintaining excess capacity, in steel production for example, dumping these state-subsidised products cheaply on other countries forcing their producers out of business, the DoJ at that time did not make decisions to intervene on the basis of political situation.

The DoJ for a decade before this WTO meeting has been using the rule of law through criminal case development, prosecuting those who as part of Chinese companies and government have been through cyberattack means stealing IP, trade secrets and military data to build China into a major global player.

In December 2018, the DoJ, under the leadership of Deputy Attorney General Rod Rosenstein, unsealed an indictment that broadly outlined a campaign of many years that found China stealing US technological advances through IP theft and trade secrets from a wide variety of industries, which had assisted the Chinese government in eroding the US military's pre-eminence and undercut international competitors.

The role of APT10

In parallel to this indictment, a Chinese intelligence official operating in Belgium was arrested for 'training' employees of US companies to steal trade secrets and was extradited to the US. Additionally, two Chinese nationals, named Zhu Hua and Zhang Shilong, were charged with conspiracy to hack into a number of US companies and government agencies. The latter included sensitive agencies such as NASA's Goddard Space Center and Jet Propulsion Laboratory and the Lawrence Berkeley National Laboratory in California. They had hacked into computer systems, committed wire fraud and identity theft targeting a wide range of companies including telecommunications, pharmaceuticals, aviation and satellite.

The DoJ stated that the hackers were working at the behest of the Chinese Ministry of State Security's Tianjin State Security Bureau. They were part of a hacking group described in Chapter 2 of this book known as APT10, which US cybersecurity firms had identified as sending phishing e-mails that install malicious software onto the computers of their intended victims. 'This is outright cheating and theft, and it gives China an unfair advantage at the expense of law-abiding businesses and countries that follow the international rules in return for the privilege of participating in the global economic system,' Rod J. Rosenstein, the deputy attorney general, stated at a news conference.

APT10 has been very difficult to contain as it continually changes the technology it uses and its internet protocol addresses to both avoid detection and to stay longer on the systems of those they are hacking.[1]

IP is key

It is estimated by experts in the field that the US loses are between US$ 30 billion to US$ 500 billion per annum from IP theft. Most of the theft occurs through cyberattack by stealth or in tandem with willing collaborators or those unknowingly being misled or coerced.

Many of the laws in China, such as those that involve joint ventures between Chinese and US companies, build in requirements such as compulsory mergers that inevitably cause technology and IP transfer to occur. Chinese laws require foreign-owned research facilities to be built in China, which makes the stealing of trade secrets easier. Data pools are also at risk as Amazon and Apple, for example, were required in joint ventures to work with local partners in China allowing them to handle data. Chinese officials state that such requirements are made to protect privacy and for security reasons. They also insist on foreign companies giving them access to sensitive technology to ensure the safety of Chinese consumers. However, the IP and technology made available to Chinese state-owned enterprises finds its way back to the Chinese government.

There are also compulsory certification programmes that require foreign products to undergo rigorous testing. During the testing process source codes and algorithms become exposed that allow products such as medical devices and certain types of machinery to be more easily replicated. Medical devices in particular are an area that the Chinese have been keen to develop because of their own domestic ageing market and those worldwide.

A major part of the punitive tariffs the US is placing on China is to force them to sign agreements to stop the above practices that are so damaging to US businesses due to loss of IP and trade secrets. The US wishes to continue to do business with China but without such punitive losses to its industry – high technology in particular.

Cyberespionage

A report released in summer 2017 by the White House Office of Trade and Manufacturing, which was led by Peter Navarro, put forward a detailed case outlining the extent and costs of China's cyberespionage campaign, as they termed it.

The report analysed the Chinese cyberattacks on US companies and the many examples of how they have reversed engineered and counterfeited products. The report quoted a study that put the cost of counterfeiting US products and pirating software programmes in the region of US$ 600 billion per annum in losses to the US economy.

Derek Scissors, of the American Enterprise Institute, who advised the Trump administration on Chinese IP thefts in 2017, has argued that China – through its theft of IP and trade secrets and suppression of foreign competition – has diminished its capacity for genuine innovation, relying instead on coercion and cyber theft.[2]

Yet, the Chinese are very sensitive to being called thieves and losing face, or in Chinese *miansu.* Saving face is very important in Chinese culture so taking a more indirect approach can be more successful. In Beijing there have been IP courts established in which foreign companies can legally take Chinese companies that have stolen their IP or trade secrets to task. There have been a number of cases in which foreign companies have won their cases and counterfeiters have been shut down (see the case of Hongda and Honda in Ruth Taplin's book *Intellectual Property and the New Global Japanese Economy*).

Using tariffs as a means to pressure the Chinese government to change their practices and institutions can be more productive, resulting recently in China easing its stringent requirements for foreign businesses being involved in joint ventures in certain sectors or by slowly developing IP appeals courts to give foreign companies a further chance to prove their case.

This does not stop China from denying any involvement in the cyber theft of IP and trade secrets, arguing that technology transfer is a normal part of business relations, or alleging that the US has engaged in IP theft or whole-scale technology transfer from Britain in its early years.

Yet, there is plenty of evidence that China has been stealing essential data of all types, such as personal, military and technical not simply to inflate their government coffers like North Korea but to support a whole programme of economic and military domination in many parts of the world. This enables them to be able to recruit foreign spies, grab mineral resources, and compromise lesser developed countries through debt leverage into leasing on a long-term basis prime sea ports and strategic locations to further their goals of becoming the pre-eminent military and economic nation globally, returning to the days of the Middle Kingdom when foreigners travelled to China to supplicate themselves before the emperors of the ancient regime – the Chinese characters for China mean Middle Kingdom. Recent examples of gaining essential data through cyberattack include the cyberattack on Marriott Hotels and the Equifax cyberattacks to gain a massive amount of personal data. The battle to stop Huawei entering countries throughout the world by controlling 5G networks, which include the IoT, is a case in point of the Chinese government supporting a Chinese company, in this case telecommunications, through huge amounts of state money to develop a system that can be used cyber-intrusively to infiltrate and control essential communication networks.

Marriott Hotels cyberattack

The hacking cyberattack discovered in September 2018 into the Marriott Hotels chain collecting the personal details of 500 million guests by Chinese intelligence units involves theft of personal data, espionage and is related to cyberwarfare and IP breaches. Other targets were the data of millions of security clearances and health insurers.

The Marriott Hotels chain intrusion was very worrying for the US government because this is where American government and military officials stay.

The Marriott cyberattacks signalled that China had reneged on the 2015 agreement between former President Barack Obama and President Xi.

A spokesman for China's Ministry of Foreign Affairs, Geng Shuang, even denied any knowledge of the Marriott cyberattack stating: 'China opposes all forms of cyberattack and cracks down on it in accordance with the law.' He further stated: 'If offered evidence, the relevant Chinese departments will carry out investigations according to the law.'

The hacking into the Marriott computer systems, coupled with the codes and patterns used, pointed to Chinese intelligence units rather than a commercial or financially motivated hack. The latter would have been interested in the credit cards stolen but not the 327 million passport details, which includes pictures of individuals, what borders and countries they were visiting. This was coupled with security clearance forms that contain information concerning finances and what foreigners the passport holders have met with and where they travelled to. This is exactly the kind of information Chinese government agents would require to identify American spies and the Chinese nationals they were speaking to. It would also lead to Americans who may be ripe for recruitment as spies for the Chinese and, in tandem with the stolen data from health insurers such as Anthem, the travel habits of millions of Americans would be revealed.

The Obama administration was so alarmed already in 2016 by Chinese efforts to amass the personal data of Americans that the US$ 14 billion bid by the Chinese Anbang Insurance Group Co. to acquire the Starwood Hotel & Resorts worldwide was blocked by the Committee on Foreign Investments in the United States. Instead the Marriott Hotels chain bought the Starwood group for US$ 13.6 billion. However, by then it was too late as Starwood's data had already been stolen by Chinese intelligence unit hackers. Marriott became the largest hotel chain in the world but only disclosed the massive data breach on 30 November 2018.[3]

Chinese intelligence units are the most active of their counterparts in other countries in recruiting foreign spies. One common source they recruit from is LinkedIn, a website owned by an American that seeks to introduce those operating in similar businesses or in research. Sites such as LinkedIn are preferred because Chinese agents can do this from Beijing, issuing a false profile and pretending to be from a corporate recruitment agency, for example.

There are many cases of such recruitment being reported. One such case involved a former CIA and Defence Intelligence Agency employee Kevin Patrick Mallory. He was sentenced to 20 years in prison for spying for China. The FBI stated that the recruitment of Mallory took place in February 2017 after he responded to a LinkedIn message from a Chinese intelligence agent who pretended he was a representative of a think-tank.

Another well-reported case concerned Yanjun Xu who was charged with economic espionage by the DoJ after he recruited a General Electric Aviation engineer through correspondence on LinkedIn.[4]

Equifax cyberattack

On Monday 10 February 2020, US officials from the DoJ issued indictments alleging that four members of China's military had stolen trade secrets and the personal data of roughly 145 million Americans from Equifax. This occurred in 2017, targeting one of the largest credit reporting agencies in the US. The DoJ believe this theft of data to be carried out by Chinese military and intelligence units to better target American intelligence officers and officials.

In response, Wu Qian, on behalf of China's Ministry of National Defence, stated that their four members were not responsible for such thefts and claimed that the Americans were legally bullying. This gave a signal to the DoJ that the Obama administration agreement to cease cyberattacks for the purposes of stealing IP, trade secrets and personal data was no longer being adhered to.

Mr Wu also mentioned in his response that according to Edward Snowden, the former NSA employee who defected to Russia while sending many sensitive e-mails from the NSA for publication on Wikileaks, had confirmed through the e-mail leak that the US has been also actively engaging in such espionage through cyberattack.[5]

The Equifax cyberattack was noteworthy because of the scale of the hack. Equifax holds data on 820 million American consumers including some Canadian and UK clients and 91 million businesses.

The nine-count indictment accuses the Chinese military hackers who they identified as Wu Zhiyong, Wang Qian, Xu Ke and Liu Lei, who are allegedly members of the People's Liberation Army's 54th Research Institute, a part of the Chinese military, of stealing trade secrets. This includes data compilation and database designs, the latter being IP. The four accused Chinese hackers spent weeks in the company's computer system, breaking into security networks and trawling for personal data.

Geng Shuang, who spoke on behalf of the Chinese Foreign Ministry, stated that the Chinese government and military never steal trade secrets and repeated again that China is the victim of US cyberattack and surveillance.

Yet, the information stolen was never used to defraud the victims' credit cards or bank accounts, which usually points to a state actor such as China who are more concerned with stealing IP and gathering intelligence for future cyberwarfare activities.

Although the Equifax CEO Mark Begor was grateful that US law-enforcement agencies takes cybercrime seriously and does everything possible to locate the perpetrators, Equifax was forced to pay US$ 700 million (£541 million) to the Federal Trade Commission for failing to safeguard adequately their information systems and not informing their customers quickly enough. The settlement went mainly to the victims of the cyberattack.[6]

Huawei and 5G

The third major case that involves the building of communications infrastructure for 5G globally is viewed by most countries in the West as having the potential to invite Chinese access to all their technology and military plans. This is because the Chinese government has backed Huawei from its inception with massive state cash injections to allow it to develop the next generation of telecommunications, hence 5G. This is one of the most comprehensive steps in the development of generational telecommunications and Huawei is ahead of all countries globally, including the US. It supplies smartphones to 170 nations at a cheaper cost than its rivals and dominates the supply of inexpensive networking equipment globally.

The arrival of 5G means Huawei is already in situ in most parts of the world to build on its own networking equipment and up take of smartphones dominating all the networked equipment known as the IoT. This means that the Chinese government and military can gain intimate access to IP, trade secrets and personal data through Huawei-installed and embedded network infrastructure. The founder Zen Rengfei and his eldest daughter Meng Wanzhou, Huawei's Chief Financial Officer, have insisted that they are an independent Chinese company that would not give the Chinese government and military access to IP, trade secrets or personal data. This is despite Meng Wanzhou being arrested in Vancouver in the latter part of 2018 for fraud and breaking sanctions on the behest of US officials who are still trying to extradite her from Canada to the US. Many, especially those from the intelligence communities, such as the five eyes (US, UK, Australia, New Zealand and Canada) have severe doubts this is the truth as the Chinese government have invested so heavily in Huawei and continue to do so.

Huawei IP theft

Such suspicions have intensified culminating in an indictment on Thursday 13 February 2020 that was unsealed in the Eastern District of New York, in which the US DoJ alleged that Huawei had engaged in racketeering by stealing the trade secrets of six major US telecommunications companies. The IP stolen included manuals for wireless technology and source codes. The six companies were not specified but from previous court filings they most likely are Motorola Solutions, Quintel Technology, Cisco Systems, T-Mobile, CNEX Labs and Fujitsu (US branch).

The particular charges of these indictments related to efforts by Huawei and its subsidiaries over decades both in the US and in the PRC to misappropriate IP from the six US technology companies.

However, the most immediate worry for US officials is that the 5G superfast network will control communications that are already working on an IoT basis including critical infrastructure such as the operations running military bases, factories and autonomously run vehicles.

Damage limitation

The US government has been scrambling to carry out damage limitation in light of its lack of investment in R&D for 5G technology. The US has been trying to limit Chinese companies' access to their new technology and now is working to restrict Chinese access to robotics, AI developments, advanced software and even sharing research.

Coupled with this is intense pressure on European allies to not adopt Huawei 5G network equipment technology. To date Huawei will not be asked to participate in 5G development in the UK.

As the former president of Estonia Toomas Hendrik Ilves asked:

> Many of us in Europe agree that there are significant dangers with Huawei, and the U.S. for at least a year has been telling us, do not use

> Huawei. Are you offering an alternative? …What is it that we should do other than not use Huawei?[7]

In July 2020, the Interior Minister of Germany Horst Seehofer announced that Ericson and Nokia can replace Huawei for 5G and that all EU members feel the same.[8]

Alternatives to Huawei's 5G

The only viable alternative to Huawei at present is Sweden's Ericsson and Finland's Nokia. They have provided network equipment for years to many European countries but they do not have government R&D support to extend their 5G network equipment to 5G at a low price that can compete with Chinese government subsidised Huawei 5G network equipment.

A possible alternative, harnessing the power of SME companies as well, is a plan being discussed among wireless carriers that involves a common and standard architecture for both software and hardware being developed by the US carriers. This would allow SME companies to each produce a small part of the standardised 5G network equipment, undercutting Huawei's market dominance.

The Attorney General Barr expressed his scepticism of this plan but in real terms senior lawmakers from the Senate Intelligence Committee in the form of Richard M. Burr, Republican of North Carolina and Mark Warner, Democrat of Virginia in January 2020 already introduced a Bill to allocate US$ 750 million to create such a US shared patent pool system. In addition, another US$ 500 million will be allocated to support a trusted and secure 5G network equipment system globally.

Larry Kudlow, Director of the National Economic Council, reported to the *Wall Street Journal* in February 2020 that the US government was supporting the development of software to undercut Huawei's efforts.[9]

Additionally, the US has taken a number of countermeasures to secure IP. These include limiting access of Chinese companies to American technology, limiting or revoking the visas of Chinese students studying science and technology in the US and those considered to be spying for China. The US Commerce Department in May 2019 placed Huawei and its affiliate companies on a list of companies deemed to be a risk to US national security. This listing will prevent Huawei from buying American parts and technology without US approval.

The US government is being supported by telecommunications companies that view Huawei's practices unacceptable. British Telecom (BT), the largest such company in Britain, is tearing out existing Huawei network equipment after purchasing another company that was based on the Chinese company network. BT was concerned by British intelligence warnings of growing risks from Huawei's 5G networks. Vodafone Group, which is based in London, placed a temporary embargo on buying Huawei 5G network equipment.

Also, in 2019 Verizon and AT&T (American Telephone and Telegraph) stopped selling Huawei smartphones in their stores after it emerged that Huawei was using its own manufactured chips instead of using American or European chips. The US NSA was alerting telecommunications companies that Huawei was steadily replacing all parts of their networking equipment and smartphones with Chinese-made products that would mean, in real terms, that Huawei and the Chinese government would have total control over the 5G network allowing them to interfere and extract personal data, IP and trade secrets without users knowing. This would mean that intelligence agencies like the NSA could not warn American companies or that of allies such as the Europeans that they were being spied on by the Chinese government and military by inserting malware or other covert cyberattacks.[10]

Patent dispute

In spring 2019 Huawei, the biggest suppliers of networking equipment, wrote a letter to Verizon, the American telecommunications company, alleging that they had infringed 238 of Huawei's patents. Huawei was asking Verizon to buy a licence to its patent portfolio. Verizon reacted by stating that the Chinese allegations and demands through Huawei were geo-political in nature and a much wider issue that had implications for all US technology companies not just Verizon. Many experts in the telecommunications area believed that the roots of these patent demands lay with Huawei being shut out of the smartphone market in the US and that it was trying to extract revenue through patent infringement allegations. The claims included wireless technology and networking devices and could have brought Huawei over US$ 1 billion in fees.

These claims would have amounted to indirect awards as Verizon does not use Huawei's products but only has indirect use through the over 20 vendors from whom they purchase equipment that may use parts of Huawei technology.[11]

Therefore, IP theft can not only be used to avoid R&D costs by stealing the patents from other companies but also through allegations of its theft can be used to extort revenue from supposed infringers of patents.

'Wolf culture'

With all the conflict and counter-allegations surrounding IP theft, whether from the US side or Chinese side, there has been concrete evidence that Huawei tries to use backdoor channels through all its networking equipment. It is the comprehensive nature of the IoT aspects after 5G, which are linked by IoT, that presents the greatest risks. Never before has a telecommunications system served through physical routers and switches so many interconnected devices. Vast amounts of information data travel through the networks with little human intervention so that it becomes possible for hackers to tap into data without the owners of the networks being aware of such intrusions.

Huawei is known for its so-called 'wolf culture' and nothing has stopped the company from pushing its employees very hard to go any lengths to benefit company growth. This led to Huawei's Chief Financial Officer, Meng Wanzhou, being arrested in Canada at the behest of the US in relation to committing bank fraud and sanctions busting in Iran.

Huawei entered the Iranian market in 1999 and within a decade it connected 130 cities through its fibre-optic cables. By 2009, Huawei had become the major supplier of telecommunications hardware to Iran. However, soon after in 2011, because of Iran's nuclear programme, both the UN and the US imposed new sanctions on doing business with Iran. Huawei declared it would not engage in new business with Iran and would limit its business with existing customers.

However, an affidavit that was made public during Meng Wanzhou's bail hearing it became clear that Huawei used a company called Skycom as an unofficial subsidiary to maintain business as usual in Iran. She used her role as Chief Financial Officer to reassure banks such as HSBC that Huawei was not breaking US or UN sanctions. HSBC, in good faith through its American subsidiary, cleared more than US$ 100 million in transactions with Skycom in Iran by 2014 according to the affidavit.[12]

Such actions by Huawei, which are among many that have implicated it in money laundering, IP theft, illegal data collection through cyberattack and espionage that could give Huawei technological domination and the ability to control global networks through IoT, which are also connected to cyberwarfare capabilities, are the reasons why the discussions are so fierce concerning Huawei being allowed to operate 5G networks in not only the five eye countries but also in others as well.

Huawei files lawsuit

In March 2019, Huawei filed a lawsuit that alleged the US government to be breaching its constitutional rights by having instituted a law that restricted its ability to carry out business with US federal agencies and their contractors.

A Texas-based federal US district judge, Amos Mazzant, in a 57-page decision ruled in favour of the United States Congress, which included the restriction in the National Defense Authorization Act (NDAA). Restrictions were not limited to Huawei but also included another company and telecommunications firm, ZTE.

Huawei was not pleased with this decision stating after the ruling that the NDAA was providing a false sense of protection while undermining Huawei's constitutional rights and that it would be pursuing other legal options in the future.[13]

Like the Samsung vs Apple patent infringement cases written about at length in previous books by this author, these cases can rumble on over 50 cases, but the safety of American and European systems from IP theft, personal data breaches and the uses of these against them by geo-political rivals for world domination such as this Chinese case rests with being in control of 5G network equipment, understanding the IoT and how to protect it from such damaging cyberattacks as outlined above.[14]

The brunt of so many geo-political, military and IP theft purposes are borne by the current number-one economy, the United States. Therefore, the next chapter will look at the US in terms of the cyberattacks that have involved IP theft, personal data hacking to collect government and military officials details and cyberwarfare and how the US is engaging in countermeasures against such cyberattacks. Countries other than Russia and China will be brought into the analysis such as North Korea, Iran and Israel.

Notes

1 'Cybercrime by China is "unacceptable", Rosenstein says', Katie Benner, Julian E. Barnes and Glen Thrush, *New York Times* (20 December 2018).
2 'Intellectual property to take center stage as Trump and Xi meet', Alan Rappeport, *New York Times* (28 November 2018).
3 'Data breach is traced to Chinese hackers as U.S. readies crackdown on Beijing', David E. Sanger, Nicole Perlroth, Glenn Thrush and Alan Rappeport, *New York Times* (11 December 2018).
4 'How China used LinkedIn to recruit spies abroad', Edward Wong, *New York Times* (28 August 2019).
5 'With harsh words, China's military denies it hacked Equifax', Paul Mozur, *New York Times* (13 February 2020).
6 'Equifax: US charges four Chinese military officers over huge hack', Gordon Corera, *BBC News* (11 February 2020).
7 Quote from *New York Times* Tuesday briefing (18 February 2020).
8 'EU insists European companies could replace Huawei in 5G network', David Bellamy with AFP, *Euronews Online* (26 July 2020).
9 'Huawei is winning the argument in Europe as the US fumbles to develop alternatives', David E. Sanger and David McCabe, *New York Times* (17 February 2020).
10 'America pushes allies to fight Huawei in new arms race with China', David E. Sanger, Julian E. Barnes, Raymond Zhong and Mark Santora, *New York Times* (26 January 2019).
11 'Huawei is said to demand patent fees from Verizon', Paul Mozur and Edmund Lee, *New York Times* (12 June 2019).
12 'Huawei's "wolf culture" helped it grow and got it into trouble', Raymond Zheng, *New York Times* (18 December 2018).
13 'Court rejects Huawei's challenge to U.S. limits', Lam Yik Fei, *New York Times* (19 February 2020).
14 There are many books and reports covering the long running Samsung vs Apple infringement case. See, for example, Ruth Taplin (ed.), *Managing Cyber Risk in the Financial Sector: Lessons from Asia, Europe and the USA*, Abingdon: Routledge, 2016 and *Intellectual Property Valuation and Innovation: Towards Global Harmonisation*, Abingdon: Routledge, 2014.

6 United States

In the summer of 2019, computer systems controlled by the Defense Information Systems Agency (DISA), part of the US DoD, were hacked stealing the personal data of 200,000 personnel including names and security numbers. There are 8,000 military and civilian employees at the DISA but it also handles data for other individuals. Ironically, this was the White House agency in charge of secure communications for military communications including presidential calls by mobile and telephone.

Even more alarming for the agency and personnel is that it includes in its remit responsibility for military cybersecurity and organises communications in combat zones. On its website, the DISA states its mission as being '... the trusted provider to connect and protect the war fighter in cyber-space'.

The DoD would not disclose who were the perpetrators of the cyberattacks but confirmed it moved swiftly to fix and thwart further such hacks. Letters were sent to those whose data were breached by the attacks in February 2020 offering to assist in mitigating any damage and free credit-monitoring services.[1]

Who is cyberattacking the US?

There are a number of geo-political rivals that are responsible for cyberattacks that target the personal data of government and military officials, as mentioned in Chapter Five on China, to recruit them for espionage, spying and cyberwarfare purposes. Other than Russia and China, Iran and North Korea are at the forefront of such attacks.

In a possible attempt to derail talks between North Korean leader Kim Jong-un and President Trump and his advisors in December 2018, the South Korean Unification Ministry reported a malicious programme installed on a desktop computer at a resettlement centre for North Korean defectors in North Gyeongsang Province. This is one of 25 resettlement centres that are run to assist some 32,000 North Korean defectors to adjust to life in South Korea. At least 997 of the defectors whose details were stolen were notified. This caused anxiety for them as they did not know if their families in North Korea would be attacked. North Korea had no capability to find out who are the defectors from their country but this would assist them. It could also assist in re-capturing them and interrogating them about South Korea, a military ally of the US. An expert on North Korean cyberwarfare, Simon Choi, thought that this was the work of a North Korean government group of hackers who try to find the names and details of North Korean defectors and noted that another resettlement centre had been hacked the previous year.[2]

Similar to China's breaking of UN sanctions such as Huawei's breach of sanctions against Iran and using HSBC as a conduit for money laundering from illegal earnings in Iran without the bank's knowledge, North Korea has been engaged in sanctions busting. In defiance of sanctions placed on it by the US and UN, North Korea has used cyberspace to launch sophisticated cyberattacks on financial institutions in the US and through cryptocurrency exchanges to generate income.

An expert UN panel that contributed to a report on North Korean breaking of sanctions found that through cyber means government hackers illegally forced transfers from financial institutions and cryptocurrency exchanges, laundering the proceeds to generate income to evade sanctions. The use of cryptocurrencies is more difficult to detect and trace as with the use of traditional banks and is the main motive for North Korea's large-scale cyberattacks on cryptocurrency exchanges such as Bitcoin.[3]

Money laundering

Two Chinese nationals who were working for the notorious North Korean hacking organisation called the Lazarus Group, laundered US$ 100 million of stolen crypto-currency. A portion of US$ 1.4 million of it was laundered by selling Bitcoin for pre-paid Apple iTunes gift cards. US officials allege that Tian Yinyin and Li Jiadong acted as money mules for the Lazarus Group, which was responsible for the 2017 WannaCry global cyberattack and a 2018 hack of an unnamed cryptocurrency exchange. According to the indictment, the pair in 2018 hacked into a virtual currency exchange stealing currency worth US$ 250 million. The funds were laundered through hundreds of automated cryptocurrency transactions to avoid being caught by any law enforcers. It was alleged that a portion of the laundered funds were used by the North Korean government to improve its cyber infrastructure to steal funds from the financial industry in the US.[4]

These sanction-busting cyberattacks for illegal financial gain are linked to cyberwarfare for the illicit monies are used in large part to fund nuclear missile programmes that the US and UN are trying to stop. Despite Kim Jong-un entering years of negotiations with the US government to halt production and testing of nuclear ballistic missiles, he and his father and grandfather who preceded him never had any genuine intention of curbing their nuclear intentions.[5]

Ransomware

Ransomware attacks are the most prevalent of criminal attacks that not only raise inordinate amounts of illegal funds for cybercriminals but also disrupt the operations of the governmental institutions and companies attacked according to the FBI. These attacks are so effective because they use cryptocurrencies and messaging platforms that are so difficult to trace, allowing them to communicate and transact with their victims anonymously. The other problem is that the hackers live outside the jurisdiction of American law so even when US law enforcement finds the cybercriminals and indicts them they are never subject to extradition. The majority of these cybercriminals derive from North Korea, Iran and Russia where the US has no extradition treaties and whose governments either initiate the hacks or share in the breached files, which are full of useful information such as personal data of government and military officials in the US, IP, trade secrets and military information used for cyberwarfare purposes.[6]

Cyberattacks on elections

In July 2019, Tom Burt explained to those attending the Aspen Security Conference in Colorado that Microsoft had evidence that Russian, Iranian and North Korean hackers were the most active nations conducting cyberattacks.

Mr Burt, Microsoft Corporate Vice-President, further narrowed the focus of the cyberattacks to the three countries targeting NGOs and think-tanks that work with US political campaigns.

In the case of Iran, a report by Microsoft in October 2019 stated that hackers supported by the government of Iran made over 2,700 hacking attacks to identify the e-mail accounts of current and former US government officials, journalists who have covered US political campaigns and accounts that have been associated with one major US presidential campaign. Hackers further attacked 241 accounts and were successful in four cases when they used information concerning their victims' profiles online to discover their passwords. Many of these politically motivated cyberattacks are using the same techniques that the Russians had used in the US elections of 2016.[7]

Cyberwarfare with Iran

There are many points of cyberwarfare engagement between the US and Iran. In the last decade, the US has launched at least three cyberattacks at Iran, mainly in relation to halting its nuclear missile programme, to punish Iran, for example, for trying to subvert sanctions or for its covert and overt military support for militants in the Middle Eastern region such as proxy wars in Yemen against Saudi Arabia or Hezbollah in Lebanon and Hamas in Gaza.

In 2019 Iranian cyberattacks increased, giving rise to General Nakasone, head of the US Cyber Command, questioning if the cyberattacks were an effective deterrent stopping Iran. The 'Stuxnet' cyberattack that crippled Iranian nuclear enrichment centrifuges nearly a decade ago is a case in point. It destroyed 1,000 of the 5,000 centrifuges operational at the time. Iran recovered slowly and built 14,000 more centrifuges and then in counter cyberattack disabled Saudi Aramco's computer systems to devastating effect. While cyberattacks have slowed Iran's missile development, they have not deterred Iran from continuing to supply Hamas and other terrorist groups in the region with thousands of small-range rockets.

Iran's cyberattacks culminated in destroying two major Saudi oil facilities in September 2019 with new-generation rockets. The Saudis knew it was Iran because pieces of the missiles found made their origin clear.

The US responded with a cyberattack but as it is a clandestine method of warfare the Iranians may not know about the attack for years to come. Some in Cyber Command are also concerned that the relatively small nature of most of the cyberattacks issued to date means the Iranians will not fear US attacks. They argue rather than small-scale cyberattacks what is needed to deter Iran would be a major cyberattack that destroys its electric grid or shuts down Iran's major Salman oil fields and refineries.

The problem with the above strategy is that it would not be easy to carry out and even if successful it could lead to a major escalation in conflict with Iran, as well as having an undesirable impact on the civilian population. Yet, in simulations of cyberattacks that took place before the attack on the Saudi's oil fields, Cyber Command were unsure how successful a major cyberattack would play out against Iran's increasingly skilled cyberwarriors. Iranian attacks to date have destroyed 30,000 of Saudi's Aramco computer systems, frozen operations at American banks with a DoS attack and disabled a Las Vegas casino. They became increasingly concerned about possible Iranian interference in US elections.

The US cyber-arsenal is very secretive as it is not desirable to give enemies the chance to create effective countermeasures. Yet General Nakasone stated that his cyberwarriors would be permanently engaging in skirmishes in cyberspace undermining any perceived cyberattack while continuing with a physical presence such as warships patrolling the seas.

It was approved by Congress that counter cyberattacks would not need to go through a lengthy decision-making process culminating with presidential approval but allowed Cyber Command to act when necessary, much like traditional military services. General Nakasone was involved in developing a cyber plan in the event of war with Iran when cyberattacks would be used to shut down Teheran and other major cities in Iran. The idea behind this was that the cyberattack by the US would be so devastating that Iran would surrender without any physical military action.[8,9]

Iran in its support of terrorist groups in the Middle East region not only contributes physical weapons but also, in a similar vein as it has learned from cyber interference in elections, can pass its hacking knowledge along to such groups. An example of such possible hacking training could have been a recent cyber scam by Hamas against Israel. The former often acts as a proxy for Iran while the latter is a US ally.

In February 2020 dozens of Israeli soldiers had their smartphones hacked by Hamas militants posing as young females trying to get the attention of the soldiers. According to Lt. Col. Jonathan Conricus it was the third attempt to obtain information about Israeli soldiers. In this case, which was the most sophisticated to date, when Israeli soldiers downloaded the young females app they allowed access to all the information and data on their smartphones.

The female imposters said they could not speak Hebrew properly because they were immigrants to cover up the reality they were Hamas members. They would send the soldiers links to exchange pictures that downloaded malware programmes to infect the smartphones and any computer devices. This allowed the smartphone to take pictures and make recordings of conversations without the owner having any idea that this cyber spying was occurring. Lt. Col. Conricus stated that the Israel Defense Forces let the scam run for several months under surveillance before shutting it down and warning soldiers to be vigilant with regards to what messages they open on their smartphones.[10]

IoT and the dark web

However, it is once more the newly emerging interconnectedness of the IoT that signals the greatest potential problems for cyberattacks in the US. This could be seen in previous chapters of this book that illustrate the IoT in relation to Huawei and 5G and why the US is increasingly wary and is trying to block access by the Chinese telecommunications systems even in the most marginal manner.

When the IoT is used by cyber hackers who use the dark web, the capacity for damage multiplies both physically and in cyberspace.

In the US there is increasing use of IoT devices from electric toothbrushes to thermostats to lightbulbs. All this interconnectivity makes it easier for hackers to enter a number of systems. One of the devices most actively used under cyberattack, which can do great damage to homes and factories, is the internet-connected gas pump. Cybersecurity firms in the US are noting that gas pumps can be accessed remotely through the IoT.

The security firm Trend Micro has noted that the most requested hacking methods on the dark web continue to be routers, webcams and printers, and tutorials for hacking online gas pumps with logic controllers, which are not just for controlling homes but factory machinery remotely. A common method for cyberattacks on IoT devices is for the hacker to create a botnet, which is a network of devices they control. The botnet can be used to carry out Distributed Denial of Service (DDoS) that can shut down both services and devices.

The concerning part of IoT is that even teenage skilled hackers can cause damage between the cyber and physical world. In 2016, teenage hackers in the US used a botnet named Mirai IoT to shut down internet services in a number of places in the East Coast of America. Poorly secured linked internet devices can be used in stealing personal data and IP, monitoring networks and spying through a computer camera in addition to shutting down services or causing physical damage.

A countermeasure to IoT cyberattacks can be using complex passwords, changing passwords often and using VPNs (Virtual Private Networks) in their home network to encrypt traffic.[11]

Bots and climate change

The use of bots has accelerated in the US to try an influence peoples' opinions on particular matters and can be used to influence elections or other geopolitical issues that can be targeted in cyberwarfare.

Climate change has been one of the areas targeted in the US since President Trump in 2017 removed the US from the Paris Climate Accord (this has been reversed in February 2020 perhaps with pressure from European states who used the adoption of Chinese Huawei 5G technology as a bargaining chip).

Bots are computer programmes that masquerade as human beings and send messages on social media. According to a study by researchers at Brown University in the US, 25% of 6.5 million tweets during the removal of the US from the Paris Climate Accord were from bots. The high number of bot-generated tweets concerned denial of climate change and were devoid of any scientific proof. The bots were utilised to give the impression and amplify the message that climate change evidence should be rejected and denied.

Although Brown University researchers could not identify who were the manipulators behind the bots, by using a botometer they could determine which tweets were human or bot generated. They found further that bots generated 38% of those that rejected scientific findings surrounding climate change, while 28% of tweets concerning Exxon oil company were posted by bots. Only 5% of tweets supporting action on climate change were generated by bots.[12]

With a quarter of potentially belief-influencing tweets deriving from bots on an issue such as climate change, it is not inconceivable that these bots can be used to influence not only elections but also sentiments concerning going to war or persecuting a particular group of people.

Cyber torture

It is not a great leap from psychological based information and mental coercion to another unfortunate facet of war – torture. The possibilities for cyber torture are not to be underestimated as shown in a documentary entitled

'Eminent monsters: a manual for modern torture', by Bafta-winning film maker Stephen Bennett. The documentary follows the CIA-funded techniques in the 1950s that developed psychological torture that were further developed by the Scottish born psychiatrist Dr Ewen Cameron. The film shows how patients at a research institution run by Dr Cameron in Canada were subject to LSD injections, forced comas and extreme mental and physical torture. These practices on patients are no longer allowed in Canada.

Nils Melzer, Professor of Law at the University of Glasgow, is the Swiss UN special rapporteur on torture and other cruel or inhuman or degrading treatment. He has argued that cyber torture through psychological methods could be readily exploited by states that understand physical torture is banned under the UN and other international law-enforcement bodies. He believes the internet can be used remotely to psychologically torture individuals through surveillance, intimidation, harassment, isolation, public shaming and defamation. In February 2020 Professor Melzer presented a report to the UN in Geneva underlining his concerns that cyber technology psychological torture is somehow regarded not as severe or real as physical torture and his worries that cyber torture could be legitimised by states. He further argues that just because psychological torture does not leave physical marks it can lead to social isolation, severe depression and suicidal tendencies.[13]

There seems to be a good deal of merit in Professor Melzer's observations as seen by the litany of cases in which all social media can be used to bully, intimidate and isolate causing depression and suicide. Trolling, bombardment with abusive messages, often pushes the vulnerable over the edge. Such online abuse is especially worrying when the President of the United States, Mr Trump continually ridicules his opponents by calling them demeaning, humiliating names and is relentless in his abuse of targeted, perceived enemies tweeted online. It is fortunate given the possibilities of cyber torture being legitimised that the majority of American senior officials from the Pentagon to those in charge of foreign policy refrain from issuing humiliating and abusive tweets or in other social media forms.

IP theft will continue unabated as long as other countries or state-backed companies have a paucity of creative ideas and rely on stealing them rather than inventing new technology that can be utilised to good effect.

Cyberwarfare will also evolve given the no return prospects of nuclear technology and will be guided by geo-political imperatives.

Yet, understanding and subverting cyberattacks that imperil creative IP and those that further the most destructive forms of cyberwarfare is of paramount importance to the world of digitisation in which information is the new gold standard commodity.

In subsequent chapters, we analyse how increases in cyberattack affect major industries and pillars of economic infrastructure and what countermeasures can be taken to undermine such cyberattacks. To this end we look at electric power grids, the shipping and insurance sectors.

Notes

1 'Data breach hits agency overseeing White House communications', Zoe Thomas, Technology Reporter, *BBC News Online* (20 February 2020).
2 'North Korea defector hack: personal data of almost 1,000 leaked', *BBC News Online* (28 December 2018).
3 'North Korea skirted UN sanctions and earned US$ 2 billion using cyberattacks. A new UN report says', Pamela Falk, *CBS News Online* (6 August 2019).
4 'Chinese nationals charged with iTunes money laundering', *BBC News Online* (3 March 2020).
5 See Ruth Taplin, *Innovation, Investment and Intellectual Property in South Korea: Park to Park*, Abingdon: Routledge, 2018.
6 'Ransomware attacks grow, crippling cities and businesses', Nathaniel Popper, *New York Times* (9 February 2020).
7 'Iranian hackers targeted presidential campaign Microsoft says', Nicole Perlroth, *New York Times* (4 October 2019).
8 Ibid.
9 'The urgent search for a cyber silver bullet against Iran', David E. Sanger and Julian E. Barnes, *New York Times* (23 September 2019).
10 'Israeli soldiers duped by Hamas "fake women" phone ruse', *BBC News Online* (17 February 2020).
11 '"Dark web" hackers could target gas pumps', Sarah Min, *Money Watch* (13 September 2019), updated.
12 'Study finds quarter of climate change tweets from bots', *BBC Online* (22 February 2020).
13 'UN warns of rise of "cybertorture" to bypass physical ban', Owen Bowcott, Legal Affairs Correspondent, *Guardian* (21 February 2020).

7 Smart power grids

What is a smart grid?

Smart grids constitute the amalgamation of traditional electrical power networks with modern digital technology. Electrical power grids are the underpinning of any successful modern economy and ensure all manner of physical infrastructure works smoothly such as mass transport and lighting systems. To make them more effective and deal with increasing sophistication of modern cities with their growing populations, electrical power grids from which all electricity is generated have now become digitised. This makes them more efficient and safer to use but also comes with the new security hazard of cyber risk and cyberattack.

Cyberattacks can cause power outages and affect the quality of the service including service disruption. The implications of such disruption can be both economically and socially destructive. The loss of power to both homes on the domestic side and, for example, to manufacturers of perishable goods can cause untold damage. Loses can include loss of time, equipment, production, services, command and control, confidential data, privacy and security, disruption of supply chains and government revenues. The implementation of smart grids is increasing rapidly around the globe and they are in current use, for example, in the United States, Europe, Russia and India. In cyber terms they are a magnet for geo-political state actors trying to gain advantage over another country: rogue states such as North Korea and terrorists of every description let alone a wide array of cybercriminals or individuals with a grievance. As mentioned in Chapter 4 in this book dealing with Russia, smart grids are an attractive target in a war of attrition. Cyberattacks on power grids are increasing as witnessed in the second week of March 2020 with a European organisation that coordinates 42 power grids confirming a successful cyber breach on all of the grids.[1]

IP and value

Both loss of IP on a large scale and attendant loss of value pose real threats to the worth of the global economy. Cyberattacks on organisations are a serious threat to IP losses and the reputation of a company. The IoT means that in 2020 the internet will have more than 50 billion devices connected to it. This means the scope for economic loss due to IP theft, for example, requires cyber intelligence and countermeasures to increase just as quickly as the disruptive technologies are increasing. As of 2020, cybercrime costs the global economy US$ 575 billion annually. It also extracts 20% of value created by the internet, which in 2020 means that up to US$ 3 trillion of global economic value is at risk.

IP losses mean that increased cybersecurity investment costs are incurred. These include, among other countermeasures, installing additional cybersecurity technologies, introducing new procedures and policies, hiring cybersecurity experts and having more external audits. These are all essential as IP is the lifeblood of all major organisations including smart grids. There are two main drivers for companies wishing to tighten their cybersecurity. The first is a concern for keeping data safe. This can be customer information or data related to the personnel the company has hired. The second, and related to the first, is IP, trade secrets and related business assets.

Cyber weaknesses of smart grids

As advanced systems, smart grids require advanced security technologies and their subsystems need to be functional even if under cyberattack. Additionally, smart grids – often through smart meters – gather sensitive information concerning their users. Smart grids not only capture information concerning users' usage of energy, but also credit issues and other personal private data. Customers can only feel secure if their privacy of data is secured. This includes third parties who may need to work on the smart grid and are bound to contractual obligations not to pass on data.

Yet, with the IoT, smart grids allow two-way communication between businesses and homes and the energy grid. This process will make the consumer aware of their energy consumption but will also allow energy, such as excess solar energy, to transmitted back to the energy grid. As renewables grow in use, this process will become widespread. In 2020, almost all European countries including Britain have smart meters. As smart grids are used in all advanced economies, the smart grid firms will then move on to developing economies spreading the cyber risk to data, privacy issues and IP even further globally. As smart grids are data and IP driven, the risks of cyberattacks increase and the added requirement of cybersecurity measures also expand and become more costly and complex in nature.

Smart grids have moved on from mechanical ones, which makes them more efficient but more vulnerable to cyberattack. Smart grids still rely on a large central generation centre for support, which leaves them open to cyberattack that leads to damage to physical infrastructure. It is the new, complex nature of digitisation of the electrical process that leads to new vulnerabilities and ways to attack the physical infrastructure. The central storage station includes a significant number of installations of energy storage and of renewable energy-generation facilities. These exist at the bulk power system level as well as distributed throughout the network. The smart grid also holds a greatly enhanced control and sensory capability that is configured to accommodate these distributed resources and electric vehicles, which allows for direct consumer involvement in energy management and efficient communicating appliances. This is an extremely complex system of millions of nodes that are all interconnected.

Use of blockchain

Blockchain technology can be used in smart grids to provide greater transparency for consumers allowing them to track directly from where their electricity is produced. Its use allows greater direct contact between energy providers and consumers. With a blockchain contract it would simplify transactions and allow consumers who operate their own solar power systems to sell power directly to neighbours or power companies turning it into a renewable small business. In creating a decentralised system, it enhances cybersecurity. It does this by holding any information and setting rules on how the information can be updated. Blocks of data increase as new information is appended and linked (chained). It has a cryptographic hash function that can mathematically add a new hash value while obscuring the nature of each input. There is no centralised authority operating the blockchain only the participants or nodes so if a breach occurs on one computer system, the blockchain will reject this particular computer data. Furthermore, to confuse cyberattackers many of the nodes hold a full copy of the blockchain database but not all. The continuous verification process of authenticating the validity of the data is termed mining. The rewards for miners engaging in this authentication process is being paid in a cryptocurrency such as Bitcoin. The caveat for the blockchain technology is that it is new, remains largely untested and can be used for criminal activities because it is so decentralised and lacks regulation.

This means that cyber countermeasures are required to work on a number of levels to protect the interconnected vulnerabilities of the system or losses to the economy and society can be severe.

According to the NIST the benefits of smart grids include: improved quality and reliability of power, optimised facilities that do not require backup during peak load times, a capacity for predictive maintenance and self-repairing capabilities of the system, expanded deployment of renewable energy sources, reduced greenhouse emissions, new energy storage options and increased consumer choice by enabling new products and services and with a new blockchain contract. All these enhancements require new cybersecurity technologies to protect the system.

Cybersecurity is therefore an integral part of the smart grid. Without it, interlinked losses can be substantial. The scale of it could be seen in the August 2003 blackout, which caused electricity outages for up to two days and affected 50 million in eight US states and the Canadian province of Ontario. The resultant cost to the US and Canadian economies was between US$ 4 to 10 billion. There were blackouts resulting in train stoppages, bank, business and school closures, no public lighting and reduced hospital capacity that had to rely on emergency generators. Both private sectors such as businesses and homes as well as the public sector experienced severe damage. This ranged from households losing perishable goods in their refrigerators/freezers, ill health from lack of hot water to rising insurance premiums. Protecting IP may also be included in this list of costs from damage caused by such power outages.

Cyberwarfare and smart grids

One of the worst attacks within the context of geo-political conflict was the 23 December 2015 cyberattack against the Ukrainian power facility which left 225,000 customers without power and in the dark for roughly three hours. The Russian intelligence services were believed to carry out the attack. It was this incident of cyberwarfare that made other governments including the US think about the vulnerabilities of their smart grids in the event of a cyberattack from a rival power. The US initiated new investment in countermeasures against such damaging acts of cyberwarfare.

During the 2015 cyberattack against the Ukrainian power grid, which was the first known power outage from cyberattack, with 30 substations affected, an estimated 73MWHh was not supplied. It was suspected that the Russian persistent threat group called 'Sandworm' was responsible as it occurred during the political and military conflict between Russia and the Ukraine over Crimea. As mentioned in this book in Chapter 4 on Russia, the country has many government and military-linked hacker groups who use sophisticated means to attack geo-political enemies but in a manner that is difficult to trace.

The cyberattack was very much in keeping with a sophisticated Russian cyberattack using the following steps. The first step involved compromising the network through an e-mail using BlackEnergy malware. BlackEnergy is a much-used malware created by the Russian underground, which automates criminal activity and has been sold since 2007. Originally, it was a toolkit used to create botnets for carrying out DDoS cyberattacks. Second, the hackers harvested user credentials. Third, the hackers seized control over the digital control systems of the power plant by remotely switching off the substations. Then they disabled IT infrastructure components and destroyed files on IT infrastructure using KillDisk malware. Then they deployed a DoS attack on the power plant call centre. This cyberattack was coordinated efficiently and thoroughly.

In this geo-political, cyberwarfare attack the United States, being an ally of the Ukraine, was keen to understand the nature of the cyberattack and its malware. A report ensued entitled *Seven Strategies to Defend Industrial Control Systems*, written by the DHS in 2015. As the cooperation between the US and its ally Ukraine was very strong, the former was allowed to analyse the cyberattack in detail and to create better cybersecurity measures for potential cyberattacks on power grids.

Cybersecurity solutions for smart grids

One of the most important cybersecurity solutions for smart grids is information sharing when a cyberattack occurs at another energy provider. In the case of Ukraine this was relatively straightforward as the US had a close relationship with the Ukraine as a geo-political ally. The US intelligence agencies needed to know exactly how the cyberattack was carried out in this first ever major power outage caused by a cyberattack. This knowledge was especially needed by the US because hackers for whatever reason are increasingly developing new ways to attack critical infrastructure such as hydroelectric dams, transportation systems and chemical plants or oil refineries.

Cyberattacks are increasing as utilities begin using smart grids that are connected to the IoT and BYOD (Bring Your Own Device) that causes greater vulnerabilities. Solutions and countermeasures are close to those in the banking sector. As argued in the author of this book's previous book, *Managing Cyber Risk in the Financial Sector*,[2] to combat cyberattacks and mitigate risk banks need, like patent pools, to share information to create a solution shared by other companies. Obstacles to this have been an unwillingness to let it be known to the wider public that their trusted bank that they entrust with their finances has allowed a hacker to steal personal data, IP or actual savings. Power grids operate in a similar manner in that trust in them will be lost if they allow in hackers who not only steal personal data but also cause blackouts with all the attendant problems that causes from food in freezers perishing to burglaries because of a lack of lighting. Like in the banking sector, the solution is a trusted third party that can collect confidentially incidents of cyberattack and their nature.

In the US, Japan and Europe such non-partisan agencies have been developed to collect and share information about the nature of cyberattacks among competitors. In Europe, for example, the banking sector helped to create the Financial Services Information Sharing and Analysis Center (FS-ISAC), which includes representatives from law-enforcement agencies, Europol and the European Central Bank among others. Information concerning cyberattacks is shared, such as the nature of the attacks, and how they affect the financial community, new vulnerabilities, technology trends and threats, cyberattack incidents along with case studies. Such an umbrella organisation could be created to protect smart grids effectively from cyberattacks.

In the US under the Obama administration, a Cyber Threat Intelligence Integration Center was created to facilitate information sharing between the public and private sectors. This has encouraged greater cooperation between government agencies and privately-run companies to share information on a real-time basis to warn all about the latest tools used to hack into both government organisations, academia and companies.

This cooperation allows timely cybersecurity information to be produced in a standardised language to both highlight potential cyberattacks and to undermine the economic strategies of hackers. Hackers use economies of scale by carrying out similar attacks on multiple victims to obtain the highest rewards. Information sharing in real time serves to notify the community of users immediately so they all can act to prevent or undermine the cyberattack. This will prevent hackers from using multiple breaches using the same methods, which drives up the cost of cybersecurity measures for all.

The development of AI and its use to protect smart grids from cyberattacks will allow the AI learning machines to mitigate known cyberattacks leaving the experts with high expertise time to deal with new and unknown forms of attacks by hackers. Cybersecurity will be enhanced while keeping down costs of cyberattack mitigation. This would allow for automation of known, for example, malware, and cyberattacks to have automated machines to block them, dispensing with human error, which allows so many cyberattacks to be successful.[3]

Notes

1 'European power grid organization confirms "successful cyber intrusion"', Erin Ayers, *Advisen Cyber Digest* (12 March 2020).

2 See Ruth Taplin (ed.), *Managing Cyber Risk in the Financial Sector: Lessons from Asia, Europe and the USA*, Abingdon: Routledge, 2016.

3 Some of the material in this chapter has been derived from the PhD thesis of 1 June 2018 by Jacob Mendel at the Poznan University of Economics and Business, Faculty of International Economics and Business, Poznan, Poland. Permission to draw material from this awarded doctorate was granted to the author of this book by Jacob Mendel himself and his main supervisor, Professor Tadeusz Kowalski. The title of this doctorate is 'The economic perspective on the smart grid cybersecurity'. Material in this chapter was also drawn from an article written in *Economics and Business Review* (EBR) by Jacob Mendel and his other PhD supervisor at Poznan University Prof. Piotr Lis. See EBR article www.ebr.edu.pl/pub/2019_2_24.pdf

8 Marine sector

Ships under cyberattack

Ships in the maritime sector are increasingly becoming victims of cyberattacks related to both to IP theft and cyberwarfare. Shipping is the lifeblood of the global economy dominating trade; trade routes interconnect all nations that engage in commerce. Ships are also becoming increasingly digitised using the latest IT to store data, new technologies, data and advanced GPS. Therefore, it has become easier for hackers, whether state actors, pirates, military intelligence or cybercriminals, to attack the shipping industry digitally. The maritime sector by its nature holds many companies in its supply chain, which allows, as noted in Chapter 3 on Japan in the book, indirect entry by hackers into the computer systems.

It is the requirements of the maritime sector, which is more directly globally interconnected than most, that allows hackers to enter through the backdoor and exploit IoT systems. Captain Ozgur Dogan Gunes, a Turkish Master Mariner with a software development background who is based in Shanghai, hacked into two Hong Kong vessels in five minutes. Gunes obtained the password and all the data he could gather from the ships' databases. He stated that the small to medium bulk carriers were sent a courtesy call from him explaining how cyber unready they were and open to reputational and operational loss if discovered by others. Gunes noted that both shipowners had outsourced their IT to the same third party, which left wide gaps in their basic cybersecurity systems.

A survey of 6,000 active seafarers in March 2018 by the consultancy company Futurenautics revealed that 47% of the respondents had sailed on ships that had been the victims of cyberattacks, and only 15% of them had any cybersecurity training. Surprisingly, just 33% of respondents stated that the last shipping company they worked for had a policy to regularly change passwords onboard while 18% noted that the company last worked for had a policy to change default equipment passwords onboard.[1]

A report in January 2020 from PriceWaterhouseCoopers (PwC) highlighted the fact that as the shipping industry becomes more interconnected (like the IoT), it needs a plan to respond to cyber events in a proportionate and measured way. PwC further suggested that members of the board should always make security due diligence their primary concern when acquiring new software or new businesses. Ken Munro of the cybersecurity firm Pan Test Partners suggested that hackers are attracted to sectors with weakest security countermeasures. What is the point of hackers developing expensive, sophisticated tools to carry out cyberattacks on banks if they can just use an XP Windows software programme to obtain the same financial rewards through obtaining personnel data to hold their victims to ransom?

In a poll in October 2018 of *Lloyd's List* readers, only 6% of the maritime industry felt confident it could deal with a cyberattack. This poll came shortly before a major survey conducted by the Copenhagen-based trade association Global Maritime Forum, insurer Marsh and the International Union of Marine Insurance as part of its Global Maritime Issues Monitor 2018 report. This study, which was based on the research of senior maritime stakeholders from over 50 countries, found that cyberattacks and data theft were the weak links in the maritime industry. Cybersecurity was regarded as the most pressing for shipping of 17 global issues highlighted. Compared to aerospace and aviation industries, the International Maritime Organization (IMO) was late in viewing cybersecurity as a pressing need for the maritime sector. The IMO in 2016 issued interim guidelines on 'Maritime cyber risk management' but has since chosen to amend its general security codes, the International Ship and Port Facility Security Code and International Security Management Code to include amendments on cybersecurity but not new guidelines. These will not be enforced until 1 January 2021. This has left BIMCO (Baltic and International Maritime Council) and the US Coast Guard, for example, to cover maritime cybersecurity issues, which are outlined in this chapter.

The June 2017 NotPetya cyberattack was the one that increasingly focused the attention of the maritime industry on being prepared through countermeasures to cyberattack. Danish shipping company Maersk lost between US$ 250 million and US$ 300 million because of this brutal cyber hacking that closed down IT systems across multiple sites and businesses. Luckily for the maritime industry, shipping companies did not rush and spend millions on cyber solutions without carefully assessing the vulnerabilities. Below are outlined a number of vulnerabilities and solutions undertaken by shipowners and port owners.

John Boles, the former head of the FBI's global cyber operations and investigations division and currently director of global consultancy Ankara, noted that the lack of regulatory pressure in the international maritime sector has given a false sense of security. Like in the banking and power grid sectors, it is the level of lack of information sharing and the under-reporting of cyberattacks that he finds of greatest concern. However, as in other sectors, those owners of shipping companies and ports have the tendency to believe their reputation will be damaged if they are found to be victims of cyberattack, which will undermine clients' trust in them.[2]

Therefore, with increased digitisation and greater connectivity such as IoT, cyber-risk mitigation measures need to be pursued.

Acceleration of maritime cyberattacks

Cyberattacks on ships are accelerating at an alarming rate as noted by cybersecurity consultants Red Sky Alliance, which have in tandem with Dryad Global, maritime security specialists, begun to publish weekly the names of ships that have been appearing in malicious e-mails. Malware and phishing e-mails have been used most widely by hackers. The most common subject headlines to entice those in the shipping industry to open e-mail attachments and links are motor vessels (MV) and motor tankers (MT). Vessels are being impersonated with such malicious e-mails. Such spoofing cyberattacks are targeted at various levels of supply-chain companies. In the week of 25 February, for example, malicious e-mails trying to insert Trojan malware named Wacatac into unsuspecting supply-chain computer systems also contained a D variant for the first time. Hackers are developing new hacking tools each day and in February 2020 started using Maersk again for spoofing purposes as Maersk was the victim of a notorious cyberattack in 2017.[3]

In 2017, the Russian military intelligence (GRU) launched an unprecedented cyberattack on companies worldwide with Maersk and Federal Express experiencing billions of US dollars in damage. This was the infamous NotPetya cyberattack that was carried out to inflict maximum damage on Ukraine but also subjected the shipping operations of Maersk and Federal Express to extensive damage. It could be seen as part of the Russian attempt to use hybrid warfare, which combines actual conventional attacks on physical infrastructure with cyberwarfare tactics disabling critical infrastructure such as ports, shipping terminals and related IoT computer systems. This attack was also linked to a cyberattack on Georgia that shut down websites and television broadcasting. Britain, Australia and other European nations all concurred with the US State Department that these cyberattacks were carried out by Russia's Main Centre for Technology, a part of the GRU military intelligence.[4]

In 2018, a number of ports around the world experienced a variety of cyberattacks. The port of San Diego during this time period was subject to a ransomware attack that demanded Bitcoin be paid to re-open computer systems. The attack caused limited functionality to a variety of services such as access to public record requests and business services. The port of Barcelona also suffered a cyberattack and Cosco shipping was victim to a severe cyberattack linked to the port of Long Beach in California. Dr Giovanni Vigna of the University of California, Santa Barbara's Centre for Cybersecurity noted that shipping ports handle sensitive information that attracts financial fraud and spear-phishing cyberattacks. As such personnel-, financial- and military-related data becomes increasingly digitised, the greater the cyber risk. Dr Vigna suggested that shippers need to become more aware of the cyber threat and invest more in protection.[5]

Cyberattacks in the Asia-Pacific

As nine out of ten of the busiest container ports are based in the Asia-Pacific region, the region is subject to increased cyberattack. If a sustained cyberattack virus infected 15 of the major ports in Japan, China, South Korea and so forth, a study commissioned by Lloyd's notes that it could lead to US$ 110 billion in losses. At current rates of insurance coverage that would leave roughly US$ 101 billion uninsured.

The report produced by the University of Cambridge Centre for Risk Studies under Cyber Risk Management projected that 92% of the global economy would not only be unprepared but also uninsured for losses. Angela Kelly, the Country Manager for Singapore at Lloyd's, noted that cyber risk is one of the most complex and critical risks facing the maritime industry today. As the implementation of new technology and automation progresses, risk managers and insurers need to work together to plan insurance solutions.

The report notes further that such a projected large-scale attack outlined in the report would not only cause severe disruption to the ports and economy in the Asia-Pacific region but would also impact the global economy because of interconnectivity and global supply chains.

The research report estimates that losses in productivity would affect every country that has bilateral trade with the ports that experienced the cyberattack. Estimated losses would be up to US$ 27 billion in indirect economic losses in Asia, in Europe US$ 623 million and US$ 266 million in North America.

Claims on insurance would emanate from 50% of port operators, 21% of insured losses along the supply chain and 16% of insured losses from logistics and cargo-handling companies.[6]

Understanding cyber risks

In June 2019, PwC held an audit roundtable with the Audit Committee Chairs of US-listed shipping companies highlighting the need for a greater awareness of cybersecurity issues in shipping. One of the crucial issues highlighted at the roundtable was the need for a holistic, vertical team effort approach to cybersecurity measures including top management, board members, risk technology, legal, operations and auditors. This is especially needed as ships become digitised, with less manning and more complexity.

The complexity lies in particular with operations technology (OT) and the interconnectiveness of IoT, which expands the IT surfaces of ships opening avenues for cyberattack that damages critical operational infrastructure. It was noted at the roundtable that there is a good deal of OT that remains unmanaged in relation to cyber-risk issues and it was suggested that it is essential that as a minimum course of action it should be understood and monitored.

It was also noted that software developers need to create cyber-resilient software bespoke to the requirements of ships, which has different critical infrastructure than other industries. As with smart grids as mentioned in the previous chapter of this book, regulatory bodies and policy-makers have a role in such developments to mitigate cyberattacks.

Awareness training for mariners was suggested as an important initiative to stop ships from becoming the entry point for cyber infection of allied corporate networks. As with IoT, ships could be an indirect and unsuspected way to infiltrate the corporate networks they are linked to, such as parent companies that hold valuable IP and personnel databases.

Maritime industries have their own distinctive eco systems that include actual vessels, ports, parent shipping companies, supply chains and software designers that all require protection from cyberattack.[7]

IoT, as mentioned many times in the course of this book, is an especially complex cyber risk. A report commissioned by Inmarsat in 2018 noted that in the next three years shipowners intend to spend US$ 2.5 million on IoT cyber solutions. IoT solutions were to comprise the largest part of ships' IT budgets in relation to adoption of new-generation technology. Japanese companies were the foremost adopters of IoT technology while Greek shipowners were found to be the most conservative. Of 125 respondents in the Inmarsat report, 65% were found to be using IoT cyber solutions for the purposes of monitoring fuel consumption. That percentage should rise to 100% by 2023.[8]

The Guidelines on Cybersecurity Onboard Ships outline a number of cyber threats for ships in particular.

One is the activist, including the disgruntled-employee threat that can disrupt operational services and involve reputational loss. The objective can be among others, destruction or publication of sensitive data, to gain attention from the media or DoS. IP theft would occur in the first two objectives and the first and third could involve a form of cyberwarfare to obtain data concerning personnel for recruitment purposes by adversaries and using the media in a propaganda war.

The second are criminals seeking financial gain, commercial or industrial espionage. The end gain would be selling and ransoming stolen data, ransoming system operability, organising fraudulent transportation of cargo and intelligence such as finding the exact location of cargo. Again, IP theft would be part of the first item and cyberwarfare part of the last item. Stealing and selling IP can be a lucrative business for cybercriminals although most criminals after pecuniary gain do not understand the real value of IP. Cybercriminals/mercenaries would use knowing the exact location of cargo to steal military equipment and be involved, for example, in the fraudulent transportation of military equipment to illegal war zones.

The third are opportunists who carry out cyberattacks for the challenge of it. Their aim is to break through cyber defences and for financial gain, neither of which would involve readily IP theft or for cyberwarfare purposes as these types of hackers are more interested in proving themselves.

The fourth are rival governments and state actors which act for geo-political gain and espionage. The objective is to gain knowledge and disrupt economies and critical infrastructure. Both IP theft and cyberwarfare are integral parts of such cyberattacks. IP theft can include naval blueprints for military technical advancement of an adversary to assist in gaining global dominance. Ports and ships are essential parts of global trade with the bulk of global trade being carried out through maritime activities. To use cyberattacks on ships and ports would be a major disruption to the global economy.

The Guidelines make a distinction between two different types of cyberattacks in relation to shipping. One comprises an untargeted attack whereby a company or ship's systems and data are one of many potential targets. The second is a targeted attack whereby the company or ship's systems and data are the actual target.[9]

New cyber-risk solutions

A new technology has been created by the Israeli cybersecurity firm Naval Dome to protect the port of Ashdod, the largest and busiest shipping port in Israel, which is near Tel Aviv. Named Port Dome, the cyber protection system will prevent hackers breaking into the port of Ashdod's OT systems. Pilot trials have begun in early 2020 and are protecting from cyberattack the entire OT networks at the port including all access points and gateways, transport control systems (VTMAS – Vessel Traffic Management System /VTS – Vessel Traffic Service), locks and gates, berths, bridges, terminal cranes and storage facilities.

Itai Sela, the CEO of Naval Dome, explained that Port Dome will provide the highest level of cyber defence without upgrades or changes to existing infrastructure. There is no training required for port of Ashdod staff and OT systems will be able to operate as they did prior to the installation of Port Dome with the only change being that hackers will not be able to carry out cyberattacks against the Israeli port.

The chairwoman of the port of Ashdod stated:

> With the security of the world's ports and terminals vital to ensuring the supply of energy, commodities and consumer goods to market, we have partnered with Naval Dome to ensure that should a cyber event take place it does not affect the port's or our customers' operations.
>
> Port Dome is technological must-have for any automated port with network-based OT systems. Ashdod Port overcame the red tape many governmental companies deal with and is now connected to the world of innovation and technology. I am proud to lead the first port in Israel to have stepped up to the challenge bringing Ashdod Port to an advanced global standard.

The aim of using this newly developed cyber defence for the maritime trade is to prevent hackers shutting down port operations, paralysing supply chains, damaging systems that can result in loss of human life, and causing financial as well as reputational damage. The annual throughput of the port of Ashdod is 1.5 MTEU (1.5 Million Twenty-foot Equivalent Units or 1.5 million standard containers that are twenty-foot globally), the largest volume of containers for the whole of Israel.[10]

In 2018, BIMCO (the international shipowners' association) found that it could not wait for regulators to introduce cybersecurity clauses as cyberattacks against vessels and ports were increasing. Therefore, it introduced a cybersecurity clause into its charter party agreements and other contracts from May 2019. It includes protection of both IT and OT systems that are vulnerable to cyberattack. IT systems require protection against fraud, IP and data theft while OT needs cybersecurity to mitigate the effects of threats to critical systems such as navigation or hotel systems, ensuring the safety of crews, passengers and vessels.

Shipowners have traditionally had problems insuring their PC systems against cyberattack so the BIMCO clause incorporates this coverage. BIMCO has stated that liability for cyberattack should not exceed US$ 100,000 but other amounts could be negotiated during the contract stage. BIMCO represents not only shipowners but also managers, trade brokers and other stakeholders. It is an organisation that tries to simplify and influence international trade agreements related to shipping.[11]

The Norwegian National Security Authority (NSM) in summer 2019 warned of increasing cyberattacks in the maritime sector and proposed countermeasures. The Norwegian Maritime Authority has been warning shipowners and shipping companies that hackers have been using social media such as LinkedIn, Facebook Messenger and WhatsApp to install malware on e-mails and not to open attachments connected to social messages. The Norwegian Maritime Authority recommended that networks should be segmented with all physical connections between administrative and operative parts separated. The NSM recommended that ships use encrypted communications between vessels at sea and land-based infrastructure.

P&I (protection and indemnity) Club Gard recommended that all ships report cyberattacks immediately to the national security authorities and ensure that their management systems are ready to deal with cyber risks by 1 January 2021 as required by the ISM (International Safety Management) Code IMO.[12]

USCG cyberattack warnings

The USCG warned in a safety bulletin on 24 May 2019 of a renewed spate of cyberattacks such as phishing and malware targeting commercial vessels. Hackers have been attempting to obtain sensitive data such as the official notice of arrival through using e-mail addresses that appear to be official Port

State Control authorities. In addition, hackers are installing malicious software that disrupts shipboard computer systems.[13]

Another significant cyberattack targeting ships' IT occurred in February 2019 in the US. In this case, a deep-draft vessel on an international voyage bound for the port of New York and New Jersey reported that it was experiencing a major cyber incident impacting its shipboard network. Cybersecurity experts, led by the USCG, responded and carried out an analysis of the shipboard network and essential control systems. The interagency team concluded that despite the malware having greatly degraded the functionality of the onboard computer system, essential vessel control systems had not been impacted. Yet, the interagency response team found that the ship was operating without effective cybersecurity countermeasures in place, which exposed critical vessel control systems to a number of major vulnerabilities. Prior to this cyberattack, the cybersecurity risk presented by the shipboard network was well known to the crew. Therefore, most crewmembers refrained from using onboard computers to check personal e-mails, make online purchases or to check their bank accounts. Yet, the shipboard network was used for everyday administrative business such as updating electronic charts, managing cargo data and to communicate with shore-side facilities, pilots, agents and the Coast Guard. It is not known whether this particular vessel was representative of the current state of cybersecurity aboard deep-draft vessels. However, it gave rise to concerns as to whether navigation systems and electronic charting were being protected by adequate cybersecurity countermeasures, if at all. The USCG found that protecting these systems with cybersecurity measures is as essential as controlling physical access to the ship or performing routine maintenance on traditional machinery. The USCG issued a safety notice stating it is imperative that the maritime community adapts to new technologies and increasing cyber risk by recognising the need for and implementing basic cyber countermeasures. In order to improve the resilience of vessels and facilities, and to protect the safety of the waterways in which they operate, the USCG strongly recommends that vessel and facility owners, operators and other related parties follow a number of basic countermeasures to improve their cybersecurity. These include:

Segment networks: 'Flat' networks allow an adversary to easily manoeuvre towards any system connected to that particular network. The solution is to segment networks into 'subnetworks' to make it more difficult for an adversary to gain access to essential systems and equipment.

User profiles and passwords: Eliminate the use of generic log-in details for multiple personnel. Create network profiles for each employee. Require employees to enter a password and/or insert an ID card to log onto onboard equipment. Restrict access/privileges to only those levels necessary to allow each user to do his or her job. Administrator accounts should be used sparingly and only when necessary.

Exercise caution when using external media: The above-mentioned cyberattack showed that it is common practice for cargo data to be transferred at the pier, via USB drive. Those USB drives were routinely plugged directly into the ship's computers without prior scanning for malware or ascertaining if the source was trustworthy. It is imperative that any external media should be scanned for malware on an independent system before being plugged into any shipboard network.

Install basic antivirus software: It is important to install and routinely update basic antivirus software.

Don't forget to patch: Patching is not an easy task, but it comprises the core of cybersecurity readiness. Vulnerabilities impacting operating systems and applications are constantly changing making the patch an integral part of effective cybersecurity.

In the safety alert related to the cyberattack in the port of New York and New Jersey mentioned above, the USCG notes that maintaining effective cybersecurity is not just an IT issue, but is rather a fundamental operational imperative in the 21st-century maritime environment. The USCG therefore strongly encourages all vessel and facility owners and operators to carry out cybersecurity assessments to better understand and assess the extent of their cyber vulnerabilities.[14]

Many of the items of advice given by the USCG seem obvious but the need for this points to an underlying problem of cybersecurity unreadiness that exists in the maritime sector. It would seem straightforward that a USB requires testing before inserting it into ships' computing systems. Yet, as mentioned in Chapter 1 of this book a cyber incident was started by carelessness with USB sticks when a Russian operative dropped USB sticks in a car park used by American intelligence workers. The USB sticks were picked up by these employees and inserted into their work computers with the result that computer systems were infected with malware providing entry to the Russian agents to both personal and sensitive data. This one act of thoughtlessness can facilitate the stealing of IP, trade secrets and plans for cyberwarfare.

Despite all the advice on how to thwart cyberattacks, one IT security company Dualog (specialists for shipping) found in the second quarter of 2018 that after scanning a total of 19.3 million e-mails, 160,482 were identified as phishing e-mails that had links to unsecured websites while 140,010 were malware with viruses and a number of different types of phishing malware. Cyberattacks were on a global basis with hackers inserting malware through bots operating from a variety of countries. The problem has increased with the growing use of data being sent to ships through e-mail attachments.[15]

GPS vulnerabilities

Ships have had their GPS systems attacked by hackers as noted in previous books by the author of this book[16] in which a number of examples of GPS manipulation by hackers on ships have occurred. One was the practice of Somali pirates around the Horn of Africa manipulating the GPS systems of ships, in this greatly frequented waterway, to make them navigate into

Somalian waters so crews could be held for ransom and anything valuable on the ships would be stolen.[17] Another example was in Singapore in 2018 whereby a US warship, the Admiral John McCain, was manipulated through GPS to nearly collide with a Nigerian oil tanker. The latest of such GPS manipulation was seen in 2019 with an increasing number of GPS spoofing breaches taking place in and around coastal ports in China (PRC). In July 2019 an American containership navigating the Huangpo River near the port of Shanghai had ships appearing and disappearing on its electronic chart display information system screen. As it was nearing its berth in Shanghai its GPS systems lost all signals. The Centre for Advanced Defense Studies, which is a non-profit organisation analysing global conflict and security, conducted an investigation into Automatic Identification System (AIS) data in the area and found that this had been happening for months with hundreds of foreign ships being spoofed and losing GPS signalling while traversing the waters of the Huangpo River. Days and weeks of data collection that unlike traditional GPS spoofing moves signals all to the same position confusing ships, this latest cyberattack moved all signals into a circle. Spoofing is more easily detected around coastal areas because of the dense availability of AIS data.

In 2017, a number of ships were spoofed in the Black Sea. This was most likely occurring elsewhere but was too difficult to detect because of a lack of AIS data. Both GPS jamming (blocking of a satellite signal so a receiver can no longer operate) and spoofing (making a GPS receiver show a false position) are increasing and have the ability to cause confusion in a ship's wheelhouse, especially when navigating through a busy port. GPS malfunctioning due to cyberattack is very dangerous for vessels and shipping in general. The ship's master can use a number of remedies to try and rectify the situation. These are: plot manually the vessel's last-known position; switch to a primary or secondary form of navigation; log an entry showing exactly where the GPS failure occurred; use all means of navigation available to navigate safely; report all failures to the appropriate authorities immediately.[18]

Navy contractors targeted

Another branch of maritime trade that is being attacked for both the purposes of IP theft and cyberwarfare are naval contractors. Chinese hackers have been involved in large-scale cyberattacks to steal everything from ship maintenance data to missile plans.

In June 2018, a major breach of a naval contractor occurred stealing secret plans to build a super-sonic anti-ship missile to target submarines. Such a prototype would have involved IP theft. The hackers had breached an undisclosed sub-contractor with the US Navy's Naval Undersea Warfare Center in Newport, Rhode Island. The breach was so severe that Navy Secretary Richard Spencer ordered a review of his branch's cyber vulnerabilities. During an 18-month period hackers had through cyber breaches obtained access to more than five items deemed critical information to keep the US Navy with a military advantage. The Chinese military and government denied involvement but Navy officials stated the hack had all the hallmarks of a Chinese cyberattack that was seeking weaknesses in US naval defences that could be exploited through cyberwarfare means without a shot being fired.[19]

Internal threat

The demand for stealing IP blueprints for weapons and sensitive technology, often associated with naval and maritime activities, is increasing as are potential adversaries. During the Cold War period it was just the Soviet Union but now, as outlined in this book, it is China, Russia, North Korea and Iran that are increasingly engaged in such activities.

Since 2013 in the US, roughly 3,000 people have been caught by the DHS attempting to smuggle weapons and sensitive technologies such as circuits for ballistic missiles. Federal agents also seized more than 7,000 items such as jet engine parts and microchips that were to be smuggled out to adversaries.

Compounding the problem, as with all hybrid cyberwarfare attacks, is the internal enemy working within a country or shipping organisation who are stealing IP or smuggling parts out of defensive military services such as the US Navy. A case in point was a Texas businessman who was paid US$ 1.5 million to buy radiation-resistant circuits for space programmes in Russia and China. The businessman named as Peter A. Zuccarelli was working with a smuggling ring headed by an American citizen born in Pakistan. Court documents verified that Mr Zuccarelli falsified shipping documents and mislabelled the circuits as being for touch-screen computers. He was sentenced to four years in prison in January 2018.[20]

Cyberattack insurance cover

One solution for those in the shipping industry that are the targets of increasing cyberattacks is to find adequate insurance cover. Insurance companies have tended to view cyber risk as an add-on or as part of existing insurance. Cyber risk has grown in the maritime sector, which traditionally relied heavily on insurance to cope with the risks of loses at sea. Marine insurance was the first insurance of the London market and has a great deal of experience of marine accidents to be able to insure fairly and for catastrophic losses. Cyber being a new risk and threat will need to build on history and experience to gauge potential loss.

The growing seriousness of cyber threat is leading to new models of reassessment. In 2018, Tom Walter, partner at HFW's (world's leading legal advice team for marine insurers) London office warned that in the course of assessing whether a vessel is seaworthy and therefore insurable, insurers in relation to cyber cover for vessels will need to send software engineers aboard as well to assess whether the latest patches have been implemented.

HFW also carried out a six-part examination on the consequences of a GPS spoof discussed above in which a fully laden autonomous cargo vessel collides with a 10,000 TEU containership as a result of a cyberattack. As mentioned above, such a GPS spoofing attack could be caused by geo-political actors as part of cyberwarfare tactics. This possible scenario was put forward by Walter and Jonathan Goulding, Senior Associate and Mariner at HFW, who also foresaw national preceding international legislation meaning that, for example, a Norwegian autonomous vessel entering Swedish waters would be subject to the latter's regulation, which complicates insurance coverage. As cyber risks and threats move more quickly than insurance provisions it is likely that cyberattack exclusion clause 380 used by many P&C (property and casualty) insurers would not be used very much by 2020 and it would take up to eight years to have a full cyber-risk international regime in place for maritime insurance, which would by then be outdated.

Associates Henry Clack and Mathew Dow pointed to insurance implications for P&I as the safety of ports becomes a more central issue for cyber risk. While the definition of what is a safe port has been developed over time, complications for insurance arise when terminals do not share their cybersecurity measures with visiting vessels. Such legal ramifications could be seen in the San Diego cyberattack mentioned earlier in this chapter.

Another legal complication in relation to cyberattack insurance coverage concerns what is considered an abnormal, rare or unexpected cyber risk. While the *Ocean Victory* case was viewed legally as abnormal, rare and unexpected, ports such as Los Angeles, which experience at least one cyberattack per month, could not be viewed in the same light.

Likewise, the maritime industry has potential flaws native only to that sector.

Secure Shell (SSH) protocol, not mentioned above, presents such a cybersecurity vulnerability. It is largely known as a terminal screen that is used to input commands to access passwords, overrule security measures, reconfigure e-mails and upload malicious files. Hackers use SSH to deploy ransomware and to install malicious files so employees can assist unwittingly in spreading the cyberattack throughout the company including in encrypted data. If external hackers achieve such access to internal systems the results can be catastrophic. Therefore, it is essential to have cybersecurity countermeasures in place to add further security layers between systems to stop a cyberattack in an early entry point within the system.

Technological innovations need to be constantly improved and adapted as cloud-based systems also hold such injection flaws. Such systems include management applications, planned maintenance systems, crewing portals, e-learning training and cargo-voyaging-charting tracking platforms.

In the case of vessels, it is best to create bespoke solutions for work efficiency purposes rather than generic ones. However, several basic countermeasures are suggested to mitigate cyber risk and attack. These include:

1 Make sure that codes of web-pages are not allowed to trigger additional queries.
2 Keep webservers, mail exchanger records and other servers separate from each other.
3 Encrypt credentials with two-factor authentications.
4 Utilise differing passwords in each platform.
5 Filter location-based connections.
6 Keep software updated to most recent programme.
7 Maintain regular back-up whether it is OneDrive or iCloud, for example.
8 All staff should have IT cyber training and be familiar with procedures.[21]

The final chapter on insurance is unique in that the insurance sector has the dual role of protecting companies, governments and individuals from cyberattacks emanating from IP theft and acts of cyberwarfare but it can also be directly affected by these cyber risk issues itself.

Notes

1 'Two Hong Kong shipping lines hacked within five minutes of "casual" online browsing', Sam Chambers, Greater China Tech, *Splash 24/7* (2 April 2019).
2 'Maritime wakes up to cyber security threat', Linton Nightingale, The Intelligence (October/November 2018). See www.lloydslist.com
3 'Weekly report details growing number of shipping companies targeted by malware attacks', Sam Chambers, Operations Tech, *Splash 24/7* (25 February 2020).
4 'U.S. and allies blame Russia for cyberattack on Republic of Georgia', David E. Sanger, Marc Santora, *New York Times* (20 February 2020).
5 'Ports on alert as cyber attacks proliferate', Sam Chambers, Americas Ports and Logistics Tech, *Splash 24/7* (28 September 2018).
6 Material from report 'Shen attack: cyber risk in Asia Pacific ports' produced by the University of Cambridge Centre for Risk Studies on behalf of Cyber Risk Management (CyRiM) project, in partnership with Lloyd's (30 October 2019).
7 'Cybersecurity: addressing the gap in understanding between C-Suite and IT managers', David Glass (17 December 2019). See www.seatrade-maritime.com
8 This was posted on Seatrade Maritime News (UBM(UK) Ltd) on 6 June 2018. See www.seatrade-maritime.com/asia/shipowners-set-spend-25m-iot-solutions-over-next-three-years-inmarsat-report
9 Taken from the Guidelines on Cyber Security Onboard Ships, Version 3, produced and supported by BIMCO, CLIA, Intercargo, InterManager, InterTanker, IUMI, OCIMF and World Shipping Council, 2018.
10 'Port of Ashdod provides Naval Dome with its first reference for Port-Dome cyber security system', Patrik Wheater, Seaborne Communications (14 January 2019).
11 See BIMCO website: www.bimco.org/
12 'Norway warns shipping is being targeted by hackers', Sam Chambers, European Operations Tech, *Splash 24/7* (27 August 2019).
13 'US Coast Guard warns on renewed cyberattacks aimed at shipping', Sam Chambers, American Operations Tech, *Splash 24/7* (29 May 2019).

14 Safety Alert 06-19 Washington, DC *Cyber Incident Exposes Potential Vulnerabilities Onboard Commercial Vessels*, United States Coast Guard, Department of Homeland Security (8 July 2019).

15 'Dualog warns of continued spam attacks as it stops 3.5 M infected e-mails', Elaborate Communication Ref.: 18107 (5 September 2018).

16 For example, Ruth Taplin (ed.), *Managing Cyber Risk in the Financial Sector: Lessons from Asia, Europe and the USA*, Abingdon: Routledge, 2016 and Ruth Taplin, *Innovation, Investment and Intellectual Property in South Korea: Park to Park*, Abingdon: Routledge, 2018.

17 See HFW, the world's leading legal advice team for marine insurers who have dealt with 75% of legal cases in relation to losses due to hijacking and kidnapping by Somali pirates, www.hfw.com/Home

18 'Mass global positioning (GPS) spoofing at the People's Republic of China', The American Club (30 December 2019). See www.american-club.com/files/files/MA_123019_Mass_GPS_Spoofing_at_Ports_in_the_PRC.pdf

19 'Chinese hackers breach Navy data', Gordon Lubold and Dustin Volz, *Dow Jones News Service* (15 December 2018).

20 'Smuggling of U.S. technology is outpacing Cold War levels, experts say', Ron Nixon, *New York Times* (17 March 2018).

21 'Cyber could bring new definitions of seaworthiness', *Insurance Marine News* (10 October 2019).

9 Insurance sector

The insurance industry has for years trying to incorporate cyber risk and threat into its mainstream policies but similar to IP coverage it has not been successful in this endeavour. The needs for adequate IP theft comprehensive cover like cyberattack has eluded the insurance sector.[1]

A report from Beazley noted as more people work from home (and this has been increasing with the COVID-19 pandemic), ransomware cyberattacks have been growing. Over 2019 the Beazley report noted ransomware attacks increased by 131% worldwide.[2]

Given the extent of cyberattack and IP theft especially through SME supply-chain providers to large companies more intensive action is being taken. This also includes the risks of cyberwarfare, which is only very recently being acknowledged as a real threat to governments and companies.

SME cyber insurance

In the UK, which is home to the earliest insurance companies, Global Data, an analytics company, found that cyber insurance for SME companies only accounted for 34.6% of SMEs. Of those covered, just under one in four (23.9%) are covered for human error. In February 2020 alone, there were estimations by the police that there were 21 separate cases of coronavirus-related phishing attacks, which cost victims £800,000. In these cases the hackers claimed to have a list of those with COVID-19 or asked the victims to make payments in Bitcoin for the list.

The essential problem for producing a comprehensive insurance policy for cyber risk and threat is that it is so expansive including ransom payments, loss of IP, physical damage and data breaches to name a few. Therefore, many SME companies, one in four (23.9%) see insurance for human error as most likely to cover many aspects of cyberattack. Potential claims categories would include physical damage, reputational losses, BI, data breaches and phishing. One in five SMEs (18.6%) believes that staff training is the most effective preventive measure to mitigate cyberattack.[3]

Yet, it could always be the case that cyber-risk policies could be the most closely aligned to what SMEs consider to be their greatest problems such as cyber included in IP insurance, cyberwarfare insurance attached to BI insurance like they are doing with human error. Therefore, instead of an all-encompassing insurance policy for cyber risk and threat for SMEs, cyber insurance could be offered within the categories most pertinent to their business and what they would be most affected by. SME companies cannot afford the near comprehensive insurance policies for cyber and IP theft, the latter that was offered by large city of London insurers such as Hiscox. It is beyond their means so a more targeted insurance cover linked to a wider problem such as human error may be the best way forward.

Staff training solutions

Staff training may also be the best practice to mitigate internal human error such as the aforementioned mistake mentioned in previous chapters of picking up infected UBS sticks in a parking lot left by Russian agents and then inserting them into the computers of a US intelligence-related agency. As noted in Chapter 1 of this book human error is often the reason why entry to hackers is made easier in targeted companies. In SME companies, as noted in Chapter 3 on Japan in this book, the weakest entry point in a company computer network is through the SME supply chain.

In the marine sector, the topic of the previous Chapter 8, it was noted that the digitisation of the computer system networks containing many e-mail correspondences provides an opening for hackers to gain entry to essential data. The Shipowners Claims Bureau Inc., Managers of the American Club created a novel way of training staff both onboard and at port terminals through a cartoon booklet entitled *Cyber Awareness*. It explains simply through cartoon figures and humour how seafarers need to be conversant with cyberattack countermeasures, whether they be ransomware or phishing hacks. As mentioned in Chapter 8 of this book, by 1 January 2021 companies operating safety management systems will be required to include cyber-risk management practices as set out in the ISM. *Cyber Awareness* is intended to facilitate such training for seafarers to assist with the prevention of costly, damaging cyberattacks including IP theft and those emanating from cyberwarfare.[4]

Cyber insurance progress

The IUA established on 16 March 2020 a new London market committee to deal with non-affirmative cyber coverage for the first time. This move is in response to growing regulatory scrutiny of policies that either include or exclude cyber risks. The management of cyber risks has become now a priority for the London company market. The new dedicated committee is aiming to understand the details of cyber risk through collating and sharing information that is publicly available, considering the model clauses in terms of impact on different lines of business as well as analysing the interactions between bespoke cyber and other insurance policies.

Tom Hughes, the IUA market services executive, is secretary to this new committee. He noted that '[a] major cyber event could have widespread impact on a number of different classes of business'.

> Companies have been working hard to assess and control their exposures to non-affirmative cyber risks and these efforts are very much ongoing. Market conditions, changing client expectations and lack of historical data are all issues that must be prudently managed.

The IUA's new Non-Affirmative Cyber Risk Committee will assist members by identifying areas of complexity and promoting best practice across the London company market.[5]

In the US it has been reported by Marsh that 40% more of their clients in the US purchased cyber insurance in 2019.[6]

One of the problems for creating cyber-risk insurance policies that adequately cover the needs of present-day companies affected by these events has been, as Tom Hughes notes above, the lack of historical data. Catastrophic insurance or marine loss insurance have been evolving for over a hundred years providing empirical evidence of insurable incidents that can be drawn upon when underwriting insurance policies. Cyberattacks are very historically recent with digitisation of systems relatively new so data on cyber risk can only be understood once enough data are collected to understand both the circumstances and the actual market values of such losses. Valuation is the most difficult and complex area of underwriting insurance claims. The different methods of valuation are varied and often do not follow an established system of quantification so historical data and analysis are essential to understanding claims and losses. Both IP and cyberwarfare are complex and the values inherent in them are not fully understood.[7]

Insurance cryptoassets

Cryptoassets are another area difficult to insure as it is so new and has little historical data to draw on when valuing it for underwriting purposes. Even less than IP and cyberwarfare and cyber risk in general, there is less than 0.5% of capacity in the global insurance market to cover the value of cryptoassets.

Why are cryptoassets so important to the cyber-risk insurance market? It is because Bitcoin and other cryptocurrencies are increasingly being used in ransomware and other forms of cyberattack as mentioned in this book. Rogue nations such as North Korea and Chinese intelligence operatives in cyberattacks such as NotPetya will only agree to unfreeze computer systems if ransoms are paid in cryptocurrencies. This is because such currencies are not regulated by any authority and are very difficult to trace. They are used in IP theft and in acts of cyberwarfare.

Evertas is the world's first cryptoasset insurance company with a large UK presence. Evertas has estimated that the current market is about US$

200 billion in total but will grow to US$ 1 trillion in the next five years as institutional investors increase their exposure to the market. Evertas has also estimated that the value of crypotoassets held by institutions is roughly US$ 75 billion but predicts that over the next three years this will rise to over US$ 135 billion.

Evertas believes the lack of insurance availability for cryptoassets is for three reasons. One is the relatively small size of the cryptoasset market compared to other sectors. Two is the lack of underwriting experience as this is such a new sector with little historical data and therefore little underwriting expertise. Three is that it is not encouraged by regular markets to write insurance policies in the cryptospace. There is a good deal of negative recent data that links cryptoassets to criminal activity.

To establish and expand cryptoasset insurance Evertas has announced plans to launch a Managing General Agent (MGA), which specialises in cryptoasset theft and loss coverages. A MGA is a specialised form of broker or agent that has been granted underwriting authority by an insurer in addition to being able to administer programmes and negotiate contracts for an insurer. Such activities include underwriting and pricing, settling claims and appointing regional retail agents. The MGA manages all or part of the insurance business of an insurer, acting as an agent or broker for them while working as the intermediary between insurers, agents and insureds.

Raymond Zenkich stated:

> We hold a unique position in the sector today as we are the only company focused exclusively on the underwriting of cryptoassets and insurance for institutions such as custodians/exchanges, traditional financial institutions, cryptofunds, traditional funds, market utilities, and family offices.[8]

In trying to cover insurance risks for a wide variety of institutions traditional and modern, it seems as if they are trying to institutionalise cryptocurrencies as well.

Governance and standards

The problem of cryptocurrencies is that because they are non-institutional and not formally regulated it is difficult to value losses that can be measured against benchmarks supplied by national government standard-setting bodies. The efficacy of blockchain, Bitcoin and other cryptocurrencies is being challenged as the regulatory authority is either absent or too nebulous to account for what constitutes the value of cyberattack losses such as theft or other damage either physical to computer systems or through ransomware or the installation by hackers on the victims' computer network systems of malware. Too often, cryptocurrencies are used by hackers, geo-political cyberattackers and criminals as mentioned in this book to money launder, for example, as it is harder to trace. How can insurance account for such cyber risk unless it can adhere to standardised benchmarks?

On 9 July 2018 the Association for Cooperative Operations Research and Development (ACORD), the global standards body for the insurance industry, released the Cyber Data Breach Standard, which constitutes the insurance industry's first standard for the breach of cyber data. This pioneering standard, which will promote both efficiency and effectiveness in the world's insurance value chain, was developed in tandem with Beazley and Aon. The former is a specialist insurer providing global underwriting and claims services while the latter is another major insurance company dealing with risk, retirement and health solutions.

This Cyber Data Breach Standard has been created in a timely manner as nearly 60% of insurers according to a 2017 ACORD/NAIC (National Association of Insurance Commissioners) insurance survey have viewed the lack of uniform data standards and forms as the main obstacle to the development and growth of cyber-risk insurance policies. There has been increasing demand growing with the rise in related cyber risk, threats and IP theft/cyberwarfare through cyberattacks, which has led to this streamlined, standardised, cyber-risk data exchange. As mentioned in previous chapters of this book, there is a need for reliable communication between organisations, in this case, insurance. The ACORD Cyber Data Breach Standard facilitates accurate, speedy data exchange for stakeholders in a variety of businesses throughout the insurance value chain including brokers, carriers, agents and software providers.

This new ACORD standard takes the need for standardised cyber risk data exchange further by increasing operational efficiency and effectiveness for those stakeholders experiencing cyber risks while establishing a baseline for compliance and audit-related activities. It also allows solution providers to leverage standards for increased support.

The introduction of GDPR in 2017 put more pressure on companies and their insurers as claims increased sharply as all manner of hackers including government-backed intelligence agencies, geo-political rivals, companies globally interested in stealing IP, blueprints and trade secrets and those state actors involved in stealing military secrets to advance their dominance globally, realised a premium was being placed on private data. Companies have faced increasing reputational losses and pecuniary ones. GDPR has given incentive for companies to report data breaches and attempts at extortion by hackers through ransomware cyberattacks, which will give rise to more claims by companies to their insurers as well as from rising numbers of shareholders suing their companies for loss of personal data and privacy.

The establishment therefore of the ACORD Cyber Data Breach Standard has assisted companies in information sharing during risk assessment and policy workflow. As increasing numbers of insurance leaders contribute to such standards, the greater the benefit in mitigating cyber risk, threats and attacks globally.[9]

Cybersecurity governance

Without thinking through the governance implications, cybersecurity measures will never be implemented. Creating uniform standards for cyber-risk insurance is one way. The other is to have an overarching regulatory framework that operates in the interest of businesses with good corporate governance and that is an independent regulatory commission in its own right.

The wisdom of this regulatory policy when dealing with cyber risk, which impacts insurance policies and premiums, is shown in the US SEC (Security Exchange Commission), which is an independent agency of the federal government. It is primarily responsible for enforcing the federal securities laws and regulating the securities industry including the electronics securities markets in the US. Cybersecurity guidance released on 12 March 2018 made it clear that public companies must have effective and apposite disclosure controls. Procedures must be in place that accurately record cybersecurity events in a timely manner. The guidance also encourages companies to consider how their policies, procedures and controls prevent trading on the basis of non-public information (insider trading) related to cybersecurity risks and incidents. Although the guidance does not introduce novel concepts and expectations, it encourages companies to both assess and tighten their existing disclosure policies, controls and procedures to ensure that they effectively address cyber-related matters.[10]

The SEC has been known for its very stringent regulation and fines for those breaching its financial security market rules so such guidance should encourage companies to revise their cyber risk measures where appropriate.

A further example whereby the SEC is providing guidelines and is encouraging US securities companies to assess and deal with cyber risk is through their reports. The SEC issued a Report of Investigation on 16 October 2018 to highlight the cyber threat of spoofed or manipulated electronic communications. It urged reporting companies to tighten and adjust their internal accounting controls in accordance with the current risk environment. The SEC investigated nine listed companies at this time in a range of different industries that were targets of fraudulent e-mails from fake executives or vendors. The investigation concerned determining whether the companies violated federal securities laws by failing to maintain adequate internal controls. Each company was cyber defrauded of at least US$ 1 million and two of over US$ 30 million. Federal securities laws demand that public companies maintain internal accounting systems that ensure all transactions are authorised and scrutinised with management's general or specific authorisation. While the companies that were targeted by hackers had procedures in place and updated vendor data, there existed weaknesses in policies, procedures and management of human vulnerabilities that were exploited by hackers rendering any safeguards ineffective. In this case, the SEC did not take action against these companies as they attempted after these cyberattacks to improve authorisation procedures and verification requirements for vendor information change.

The companies also bolstered account reconciliation procedures and outgoing payment notification. Finally, they provided staff with training concerning relevant threats in addition to policies and procedures to mitigate such cyber threats. The SEC in this case emphasised to these companies the necessity of having internal control systems that factor in both cyber-related threats and human error.[11]

Insurance company digitalisation

Insurance companies which are part of the city of London market have been relatively slow to incorporate digitalisation processes that are required both for the digital age and to deal with cyber risk, threat and cyberattack. Lloyd's of London, the oldest and largest syndicate insurance companies in the city of London, which has its roots in a coffee house opened by Edward Lloyd in 1686 where shipping merchants exchanged shipping intelligence, carried out a digitalisation drive. DBRS Morningstar released commentary on this procedure and contrasted it with the Association of Bermuda Insurers and Reinsurers. The commentary pointed to a number of policy measures by Lloyd's to re-organise its business into a digital one. One such policy measure concerns Lloyd's laying the groundwork from plans set out in May 2019, which should show results in the first quarter of 2020. It was a six-month thinking through the transition process that aimed to both strengthen and expedite insurance risk protection services to clients while increasing the ease of doing business through digitalisation and reducing costs. It is an attempt to bring Lloyd's into the digital age allowing it to compete with other large insurance markets that have lower expenses.

DBRS Morningstar has noted that Lloyd's is making progress in its strategy to digitalise, innovate and expedite needed changes that will be clarified after the first quarter of 2020. These changes to progress digitalisation are necessary to improve efficiency in the insurance underwriting business while increasing competitiveness in the lower cost insurance market. Lloyd's has through these measures been closing down underperforming syndicates and raising prices.[12]

Lloyd's of London has had a few problems related to its website, which was not updated. The PRA had Lloyd's placed on special measures in December 2019, as it emerged that a whistleblowing hotline for staff to report misconduct and fraud anonymously had been unusable for 16 months. Additionally, the e-mail and telephone numbers on its websites for members to submit complaints about agents were left unattended for weeks as the contact details were out of date.[13]

In the author of this book's estimation, such re-organisation of large, cumbersome, paper-based insurance companies is sorely needed to ensure that they can provide cyber-risk insurance of a high standard that is relevant to the current situation of increasing cyberattacks that include IP theft and cyberwarfare. Without digitising their own company, they cannot underwrite adequately cyber risk and institute their own cyber threat countermeasures that will prevent their own organisations from becoming victims of cyberattack and losses. Lloyd's digitisation process has been reaping results on the back of their 2018 annual report, which showed that they underwrite roughly a third of the global cyber-risk market share, which mainly derives from the US market.

Cyberwarfare insurance

Cyberwarfare, as mentioned in previous chapters of this book, is in ascendancy using cyberattack for both physical targets and non-physical ones. Targets include power grids, shipping and military installations and personnel. This is such a new cyber risk that insurance companies have only begun to think about the risks that need protecting and the values inherent in underwriting such cyber losses. Many experts in the insurance industry note that more consensus and consistency are necessary before the insurance industry can arrive at workable solutions.[14]

Cyber risk – the top peril for insurance

For the first time cyber risk has become the main peril judged by companies worldwide according to the Allianz Risk Barometer 2020. In the Ninth Allianz Risk Barometer, 39% of respondents for the first time viewed cyber incidents as the number one business risk, relegating the usual top business peril of BI to second place with 37% of respondents. Given the growing reliance of companies on IT and data, awareness has been increasing in recent years of cyber threat through numerous cyber incidents. Just seven years ago cyber risk ranked 15th among 6% of respondents. The survey incorporates the views of 2,718 experts including CEOs, risk managers, brokers and insurance experts. Other than cyber risk, the top concerns that have gained prominence in the 2020 survey include changes in regulation and legislation at number three with 27% and climate change at number seven with 17% of respondents.

Joachim Muller, the CEO of AGCS, noted that the 2020 Barometer pointed to the fact that cyber risk and those risks associated with climate change are the most significant threats to global business. He stated:

> Of course, there are many other damage and disruption scenarios to contend with, but if corporate boards and risk managers fail to address cyber and climate change risks this will likely have a critical impact on their companies' operational performance, financial results and reputation with key stakeholders. Preparing and planning for cyber and climate change risks is both a matter of competitive advantage and business resilience in the era of digitalization and global warming.

Cyber risk is viewed not only as the top risk globally but also among the three most important risks in countries such as Austria, Belgium, France, India, South Africa, South Korea, Spain, Sweden, Switzerland, the UK and the US. The rate of data breaches is increasing with ransomware and spoofing being among the most common cyberattacks. In conjunction with the frequency of cyberattacks comes privacy-related fines as mentioned in relation to GDPR above and to increased litigation. A large data breach that involves over 1 million compromised records costs on average US$ 42 million, which is up 8% year on year.

As mentioned above, the cause of many cyber incidents are related to human error. Often hackers are given entry into the computer systems of companies through ignorance, carelessness or in some cases employee grudges.

Marek Stanislawski, Deputy Head of AGCS noted: 'Many incidents are the results of human error and can be mitigated by staff awareness trainings which are not yet a routine practice across companies.'

Business interruption

After seven years, BI, is no longer at the top of company priorities, but in second place it still constitutes a great concern according to the Allianz Barometer. In fact, as noticed in this book, BI risk has expanded and diversified. With cyberwarfare and physical damage to infrastructure occurring more frequently through cyberattack mechanisms, BI has become more complex and profound.

Raymond Hogendoorn, Global Head of Property and Engineering Claims at AGCS, says:

> Digital supply chains and platforms today allow for full transparency and traceability of goods but a fire at a data center, a technical glitch or a hack could bring large BI losses for multiple companies that all rely and share the same system and which cannot switch back to manual processes.

State-supported terrorism such as ISIS, rogue state missile damage such as from North Korea, which is missile testing once again in March 2020, to cyberattacks on power grids that make them unworkable all feed BI. Insurance underwriters are being required to expand their definition and cover for cyber risk.

Changes in regulation and legislation ranked third and much of the risk is related directly to trade war disputes as between China and the US. This type of risk is directly related to IP and trade secret theft. In 2019 about 1,300 trade barriers were initiated. As it becomes increasingly part of geo-political influence and rivalry between states, cyberattack in general and cyberwarfare will grow in importance as insurable risks. New regulatory changes such as those inspired by climate change will accelerate the need for new definitions of cyber risk.

Climate change is in the top three business risks for the Asia-Pacific region. Businesses are increasingly worried about physical damage caused by climate change. In the Allianz Risk Barometer 49% of respondents expressed such concerns. Extensive flooding, droughts that cause fire damage and fierce storms all cause damage and pose threats to factories, corporate physical assets and supply chains. Operational disruptions that lead to relocation of facilities all constitute greater risk. Litigation is increasing in relation to carbon issues, especially in the US, which complicates insurance underwriting and places greater pressure on the role of risk managers.[15]

Cyber-risk assessment is so important to insurance underwriters because cyber threat and attack are increasingly causing the risk and damage for insurance claims. It is also important for insurers in general as they are becoming the target of hackers. US insurer Chubb, which is a major player in the cyber insurance market, seems to have been the target of a ransomware attack.[16]

Future issues for cyber insurance

Standardisation of policy wording

A present and future challenge to the assessment of the outcome to such scenarios is the standardisation of policy wordings. A danger to both such standardisation and assessing such scenarios is not having clear, robust exclusions and also ambiguity of wording, which allows for many different interpretations.

The author of this book, when having an IUA-supported book launch of her *Managing Cyber Risk in the Financial Sector* book in 2016, noted in her presentation and in her book that a lack of rigorous use of standardised language only leads to unsatisfactory cyber-risk underwriting as in the end neither the insurers nor the insureds understand fully for what they are being covered. This is especially the case in cyber IP theft where the cyber risk is complicated by the sophistication of valuing the worth of IP and in many cases the theft of trade secrets.

Silent cyber vs affirmative

There is a growing challenge of silent cyber/non-affirmative or unintended/affirmative insurance policies. The first refers to non-inclusion of cyber liabilities either unintended or intended and the latter to inclusion.

The first category refers to cases in which cyber risks and threats are not explicitly excluded or included. When included, the language used is ambiguous and the insurer did not price in or even contemplate loss scenarios due to cyber threats and attacks. These omissions in cyber coverage can be related to property such as BI and errors and omissions liability such as covering human error when securing data. Other areas can concern directors or officers who require indemnification in the event of breaches because adequate protocols or procedures were not in place or general liability in which property damage, bodily harm or breach of privacy occurs. An example of the latter is that a cyberattack targets a building's elevators causing physical damage to the system and bodily harm when the people inside the elevator fall when it jerks as it stops. This means that unknown or unquantified exposures because of cyberattack result in liabilities that are linked to traditional property or liability coverage.

Affirmative (the second category) refers to inclusion of cyber risks and threats/attacks in stand-alone network and security private policies. These can also take the form of endorsements added to P&C policies that cover the costs linked to data breach and network security failure because of cyberattack. Common coverages can include first and third party. First-party coverage can be in relation to event management/breach response for call centres, forensics, public relations or credit monitoring services; BI losses and expenses; and cyber extortion and ransomware where payments, for example, are demanded to re-open computer systems. Also included would be costs associated with data restoration. Third-party coverage would be in the case of privacy liabilities such as failure to prevent unauthorised access/disclosure of confidential information and fines and penalties associated with this. Network security liability is another area that concerns failure to prevent or employ countermeasures to stop an attack on computer systems. The third area is privacy regulatory defence costs, which is where a privacy breach may be subject to regulatory fines or penalties. First-party cyber liabilities were clarified after the devastating 2017 NotPetya and WannaCry attacks. NotPetya, in particular, aided clarification because ransomware and BI losses went over the billion-dollar benchmark.

The PRA believes that UK insurers should be able to assess their non-affirmative exposure more accurately. Companies with the most developed approaches are those that can analyse and bring together different parts of their organisation.

Lloyd's is seeking to make every policy written by a Lloyd's market participant either provide affirmative cyber coverage or exclude cyber coverage explicitly.

The global insurance market is concerned about cyber coverage because losses could outstrip incoming premiums if silent cyber is not dealt with adequately. A study by Guy Carpenter and CyberCube in 2019 estimated that the US industry within a 1-in-100 return period produces a yearly total of cyber-catastrophe insured losses of US$ 14.6 billion. This estimate can include one or more incidents within the same year. This was based on the US stand-alone cyber insurance industry.[17]

Cyber insurance stress tests in the UK according to a PRA survey in 2018 show that gross losses could outstrip cyber premiums several times over. This estimation did not include silent cyber. The PRA survey suggested that a cyber catastrophe could substantially alter the dynamics of the market. Yet, even without a major cyber event, demand from all quarters could push premiums into US$ billions.

Insurers —— the new 'hated' bankers

With the COVID-19 pandemic raging and insureds clamouring for cover, insurance companies are concerned that they will become the focus of public backlash – the fate that befell the banking community after the 2008 financial crisis.

The message from many insurance companies that they will not pay out for lost business or abandoned travel costs is viewed as a lack of empathy with problems insureds face when compared to other business sectors such as banks, which are offering mortgage 'holidays'. By comparison, insurance companies are seen as greedy as they face an avalanche of complaints from those insureds who find they are not covered for critical illness, travel disruption and BI because of cyberattacks. Insurers will not pay out for BI because most companies buy for day-to-day risks such as flood and fire. Insurers are in difficulties themselves as policies did not price in pandemics so they have not been able to create reserves to be able to pay out. Executives have stated that they are trying to assist customers through policy payment holidays and advice giving but acknowledge that creating policies to cover the risk of such devastating pandemics are beyond the scope of any domestic insurer.[18]

As the fallout grows from COVID-19 cyberattacks mentioned above and the global pressures of the pandemic, the insurance industry may also have to prepare for cyberwarfare.

Notes

1 See Ruth Taplin, *Managing Cyber Risk in the Financial Services: Lessons from Asia, Europe, and USA*, Abingdon: Routledge, 2016.
2 'Ransomware attacks rise 131 percent, threaten home workers: Beazley', Erin Ayers, *Advisen Cyber News, Digest Edition* (26 March 2020).
3 'Majority of UK SMEs are vulnerable to cyber attacks says Global Data', material based on Ben Carey-Evans, Financial Services Analyst at Global Data, Global Data Press Release (10 March 2020).
4 See www.american-club.com/page/comics
5 'IUA members focus on non-affirmative cyber coverage', media release by Scott Farley, Director of Communications, IUA (16 March 2020).
6 'Marsh reports more than 40 percent of U.S. clients bought cyber insurance in 2019', Chad Hemenway, *Advisen Cyber News, Digest Edition* (26 March 2020).
7 See Ruth Taplin, *Valuing Intellectual Property: Towards Global Harmonisation*, Abingdon: Routledge, 2015.
8 'World's leading cryotoasset insurance company announces plans to become a managing general agent', Phil Anderson of Perception A for Evertas (25 March 2020).

9 'ACORD, Aon, and Beazley unveil industry's first standard for global cyber data breach', ACORD press release, Peral River, New York, USA (9 July 2018).
10 'New SEC cybersecurity guidance: focus on governance', Hannah Scott, AIG Public Relations (12 March 2018).
11 SEC February 2018 Guidance and SEC Report of Investigation, 16 October 2018.
12 'Lloyd's new strategy: embracing digitalisation to drive efficiencies and business transformation', commentary by DBRS Morningstar, 24 February 2020.
13 'Complaints system failure increases pressure on Lloyd's of London', Ben Martin, *The Times* (9 March 2020).
14 'Is cyber warfare insurable? The industry is working on it', Erin Ayers, *Advisen Cyber News*, *Digest Edition* (13 February 2020).
15 'Allianz Risk Barometer 2020: cyber top peril globally for the first time', Jonathan Tilburn, Press Contact, Allianz, London/Munich (14 January 2020).
16 'Insurer Chubb investigating cyber incident: network remains fully operational', Chad Hemenway, *Advisen Cyber News*, *Digest Edition* (30 March 2020).
17 'Looking beyond the clouds: a U.S. cyber insurance industry catastrophe loss study: 2019', Guy Carpenter, Marsh and McLennan Companies document. See www.cybcube.com/wp-content/uploads/2020/01/Beyond-the-Clouds.pdf
18 'Insurers fear they will join bankers as hate figures', Katherine Griffiths, *The Times* (23 March 2020).

10 Conclusion

Future considerations

COVID-19 future cyberattacks

The global pandemic caused by coronavirus or COVID-19 that began in Wuhan in China through eating wild animals that harbour coronavirus from an unhygienic, live wildlife food market has ravaged the global economy and now global health. Can it cause even greater problems for the global economy and social situations such as the potential cancelling of the Tokyo Olympics, which would cause further damage to the Japanese economy? It seems it can and in relation to cyber risk, threat and attack.

As unprecedented numbers of people are working from home, the problems of maintaining adequate cybersecurity are burgeoning. Phishing attacks have risen by 667% in the UK since the start of March 2020. This estimation was based on calculations by the security firm Barracuda Networks, which saw the 137 coronavirus phishing e-mails identified in January 2020 and the 1,188 in February 2020 explode to 9,000 in March 2020. These phishing attacks are the work of malicious hackers who are bombarding home-based workers with coronavirus alerts from fake charities purporting to stop the spread of the virus. The alerts are sent by hackers who try to extort information or money from recipients. Despite this, according to Barracuda Networks the 467,825 COVID-19 related phishing e-mails only account for 2% of cyberattacks worldwide from the beginning of March 2020.[1]

Yet, as COVID-19 continues, the scale and amount of cyberattacks in all their forms as mentioned in this book are increasing in scope and potential for damage. Working from home accelerates the potential for cyberattack as home computers often lack the security measures exercised and available in the workplace. This can facilitate further stealing of IP and cyberwarfare-related cyberattacks that target the names and particulars of military personnel and can cause infrastructural damage.

Cyberattacks increase but so does future awareness

According to statistics from the UK Department for Digital, Culture, Media and Sport (DCMS), nearly a half of businesses in Britain have experienced a cyberattack that attempted to or breached their security measures. This was for the past 12 months from March 2019, with 68% of SMEs and 75% of large companies being the target of cyberattacks.

The 2019 DSMC report noted that the increase in cyberattacks is most likely linked to an increase in cybersecurity awareness. Out of the 46% that stated they were being subject to cyberattack, the majority noted that they were being hacked once a week, which showed a 32% awareness compared to 22% in 2017.

The nature of cyberattacks is shifting towards phishing e-mails from 72% in 2017 to 86% in 2020 accompanied by a fall in viruses and malware from 33% to 16%. Yet, phishing cyberattacks are often made in tandem with malware.

Over the past five years more management board members of companies are becoming involved in instituting cybersecurity countermeasures.

The DSMC report found that 80%, compared to 69% in 2016, of senior management now viewed cyber risk and security as top priorities. It found that more businesses were proactive in finding out information concerning cybersecurity measures from the NCSC. They believe this has been driven by GDPR concerns, which have been discussed in this book in a number of chapters.

The DSMC report noted, however, that a good deal more work is needed in relation to external and internal security audits with only half of businesses carrying them out in the past 12 months and quality varying a great deal.

Insurance take up to cover cyber risk, threat and attack still remains quite low at 32%. Some of the reasons for this have been outlined in Chapter 9 of this book on insurance.

The 2019 DSMC report noted that the average or mean cost to the UK businesses surveyed of cyber incidents was £3,230 for small businesses and £5,220 for medium and large businesses.

Stigma of reporting diminishing in future

Reactions to the DCMS report largely point to the fact that the stigma faced by many companies in relation to reporting publicly cyberattacks is beginning to abate. As mentioned many times in this book, whether it is Japan the US, the UK or Europe in general, one of the major impediments in dealing with cyber risk has been the fear of companies that if they report that they have been successfully hacked it will expose them to loss of reputation and they will lose customers and customer confidence. Now that so many companies large and small have been reporting their cyberattacks and the regulatory framework is levelling fines while at the same time rewarding them for reporting, the stigma is now diminishing. The stigma related to reporting has also decreased because governments are also having to report because of sheer numbers of increasing cyberattacks.

Charities are also increasingly bearing the brunt of cyberattacks and so are cloud services, which are supposed to protect against data breaches. Therefore, the emphasis is changing towards greater interest in how companies can find the best countermeasures to mitigate cyber risk, threat and attack and how to best train staff in implementing countermeasures.

Yet, as mentioned many times in this book it is not the technology that is failing companies and those, for example, who use cloud platforms such as Amazon Web Services that provide good cybersecurity measures. It is instead human error that allows the cyberattacks to occur because staff who are managing the countermeasure systems do not understand them well enough. The knowledge gap between understanding the need for cybersecurity measures to be intact needs to be matched by the equally important requirement of skilled experts to operate such cyber mitigation systems. When this gap closes and all businesses view reporting cyber incidents as an effective and efficient method of fighting cyber risk and as a matter of routine, countering cyberattacks will become much more efficacious.[2]

Future insurance solutions

Willis Towers Watson (NASDAQ: WLTW), with roots dating back to 1828 in London, is a major global advisory, broking and solutions company that employs 45,000 people in 140 countries. Its announcement on 28 April 2020 of the launch of CyNav highlights future developments in sectoral cyber insurance cover. In this case it is a new type of cyber insurance cover designed specifically for marine sector shipowners.

The new cyber insurance product addresses the increasing need for a bespoke marine cyber solution, built from the ground up to specifically address shipoperators' exposures, rather than trying to use pre-existing generic cyber products amended marginally to fit marine exposures. Shipowners are increasingly reliant on digital technology for all aspects of their operations and their unique risks associated with this dependency can lead to significant financial damage as outlined in Chapter 8 of this book on the marine sector.

CyNav's pioneering approach includes the following central features:

- Crisis management costs include cover that protect the rights of shipowners from the most common cyberattacks of ransomware attack and data breaches.
- BI, the second most common outcome of cyberattack, cover in the event of a cyber incident that disrupts operations (including where the incident occurs at a third-party IT service provider upon which the shipowner relies).
- Property infrastructural damage and loss of hire cover arising from a cyberattack or satellite communication interference such as GPS (spoofing).
- Loss of hire cover arising from disruption to or detainment of a vessel following a cyberattack such as pirates mentioned in Chapter 8 of this book.

Cover for fines and defence costs arising from regulatory actions, including those under GDPR and the Network and Information Systems Directive.

As the financial impact of cyber incidents continue to accelerate while the silent cyber cover in traditional marine cover is being reduced substantially, CyNav offers a cyber solution of the future, which is designed to close remaining gaps in current cyber cover.

Ben Abraham, Global Head of Marine at Willis Towers Watson, said:

> Barely a week goes by without new cyber events affecting the maritime sector. Many are minor and unreported, but the major cases have caused consequential commercial losses in the hundreds of millions of dollars. CyNav offers a genuinely pioneering marine-specific cyber solution. In an environment of increasing ingenuity of cybercriminals and increasing levels of cyber security governance in the maritime industry, CyNav anticipates the protection that shipowners need to mitigate their cyber risk.[3]

AI and future cyberattack mitigation

As human error is often the cause of successful entry into computer systems, it is possible that learning machines could be used to protect IP from theft and nations suffering from cyberwarfare attacks. This is nothing to do with science fiction or the unrealistic horror scenario of robots developing their own minds and murdering masses of people. AI is being developed as learning aids in education and even to map areas to assist with stopping pandemics such as the current COVID-19.

Slowing the pandemic

The C3.ai Digital Transformation Institute is a new research consortium that includes commitments from Princeton University, Carnegie Mellon University, the Massachusetts Institute of Technology, the University of California, the University of Illinois and the University of Chicago, as well as C3.ai and Microsoft. It is attempting to find expert scientists who can use AI to solve a number of social problems. It views the coronavirus as its first challenge.

This new institute has been seeking novel ways of slowing the pathogen's spread, speeding the development of medical treatments, designing and repurposing drugs, planning clinical trials, predicting the disease's evolution, judging the value of interventions, improving public health strategies and finding better ways in the future to fight infectious outbreaks.[4]

Cyberwarfare

As AI can be used for protective measures, such as fighting the coronavirus pandemic, it can also be used to operate cybersecurity systems that mitigate cyberattack by detecting hackers, their malware and blocking them. Such

AI machine learning systems are already in operation within the realm of cyberwarfare.

Stuart Russell, a computer scientist at University of California, Berkeley, noted that there are many weapons systems currently that use AI based on software transforming the technology already in use. The concept of artificial general intelligence that can operate on its own does not exist in practice at this point in time.

Paul Scharre, a former Army Ranger now acting as a policy analyst, wrote in his book *Army of None: Autonomous Weapons and the Future of War* that over 30 countries already use defensive supervised autonomous weapons in situations where the speed of engagement is too fast for humans to respond.

The most well-known of such weapons is the Israel Aerospace Industries Harpy. This is an armed drone that can maintain a presence high in the skies while surveying large areas of land until it detects an enemy radar signal and at this point it collides with the source of the radar warning, destroying both itself and the target.[5]

These type of AI high-tech cyberwarfare drones are not flexible but execute precisely what they are programmed to do. They are not just driven by military need but by high-tech companies that are expanding their AI products and services. This same technology can be used to prevent human error in relation to companies losing their IP through cyberattack as in cyberwarfare to destroy cyber-activated weapons out to destroy human targets for geopolitical reasons.

Future cyberattacks on IP, intelligence and AI

Future cyberattacks on IP, trade secrets and intelligence will be from China and Russia. An alliance of these two authoritarian states is one of the greatest threats to democracy globally and the protection of IPR as a whole. A recent example of the dangers of such an alliance is that of the Turbine Panda. The latter is the name of a Chinese-based cyberespionage group that carried out cyberattacks on US aeronautics companies with the intention of stealing the IP blueprints of the components for the C919 custom built engine, which the Chinese state-owned enterprise COMAC (Commercial Aircraft Corporation of China) asked the US-based CFM International to create. CFM International is a joint venture between General Electric, a US firm, and Safran Aircraft Engines of France. Between 2010 and 2015, Turbine Panda Chinese state-sponsored hackers carried out cyberattacks against multiple companies that were component suppliers for CFM International such as Safran and Honeywell.

Subsequently in August 2016 researchers noted that the CJ-1000AX engine made by a Chinese company in which COMAC became a recent shareholder produced an engine similar to the C919, especially in the turbofan blade design.

Both Crowdstrike Intelligence Reporting and unnamed US government sources concluded that China used IP theft from insiders, joint ventures, forced technology transfer and cyberattack espionage to obtain the technical information it needed.[6] The Chinese insider who carried out the IP theft worked for the French-Chinese joint venture Safran Suzhou. He was recruited by a Chinese intelligence officer who provided him with a USB drive with Chinese-developed Sakula malware on it, which the Chinese insider inserted into the Safran Suzhou computer system. This occurred in January 2014 and the two Chinese were eventually arrested but the cyberattacks have not stopped, with the goal being a Chinese-Russian substitute, which appears to be the CJ2000 aircraft engine. Can future AI development stop such IP theft?

A report by the Royal United Services Institute (RUSI) in April 2020 commissioned by GCHQ points to increasing and more sophisticated cyberattacks on the intelligence communities. As adversaries will turn to cyberspace to launch cyberwarfare attacks, intelligence communities will be required to use AI to detect and stop them. The cyberattacks will be from state actors for geo-political reasons and by criminals, both groups using AI for attack purposes. The RUSI report notes that this will give rise to further complications such as new human rights and privacy considerations, which will require new guidance on these issues.

AI will be used in a number of ways in the future. One way it can be used is to mutate malware cyberattacks. This could, first, make it more difficult for normal computer systems to detect or, second, it could be used to re-programme drones to attack the senders.

Other future uses could be to create what is termed deep fakes, which appear to be from a real person but actually is a manipulated image that could be used to persuade voters, for example, in an election to support a particular candidate.

Therefore, AI will be used as a countermeasure against malicious hackers who are trying to use it to attack for geo-political or criminal reasons. It will be less effective in use for predictive profiling, for example, of terrorists as innumerable variables will dilute the effectiveness of its usage in this application. Consequently, AI will be developed incrementally rather than be an instantaneous totally new mode of operation. Ethical considerations will also be of paramount importance in its development.[7]

Finally, whether it is deterring the theft of IP or dealing with issues of cyberwarfare, machine learning or AI will develop to be used to counter cyberattacks and hopefully within an ethical framework.

Notes

1 'Email phishing attacks rise 667 percent', Sead Fadilpasic, *IT ProPortal* (31 March 2020).

2 'Almost half of UK businesses suffered a cyber attack in past year', Alex Scroxton, Security Editor, *Computer Weekly Online* (25 March 2020).

3 'Willis Towers Watson launches customised cyber cover for shipowners', Sam Horril, WLTW press release, London (28 April 2020).
4 'A.I. versus the coronavirus', William J. Broad, *New York Times* (26 March 2020).
5 'A.I. is making it easier to kill (you). Here's how', Jonah M. Kessel, *New York Times* (13 December 2019).
6 'Security firm revealed that China-linked APT group Turbine Panda conducted cyber-espionage operations aimed at various aerospace firms for years', Pierluigi Paganini, *Security Affairs* (18 October 2019).
7 'UK spies will need artificial intelligence – Rusi report', Gordon Corera, Security Correspondent, *BBC News Online* (27 April 2020).

Index

Note: Entries in **bold** refer to tables.

For Product Safety Concerns and Information please contact our EU
representative GPSR@taylorandfrancis.com
Taylor & Francis Verlag GmbH, Kaufingerstraße 24, 80331 München, Germany

www.ingramcontent.com/pod-product-compliance
Ingram Content Group UK Ltd.
Pitfield, Milton Keynes, MK11 3LW, UK
UKHW022122190926
475702UK00013B/1598
9780367621858